Sustainability *by* Design

A VISION FOR A REGION OF 4 MILLION

THE REAL ESTATE FOUNDATION OF BRITISH COLUMBIA

Major funding for this document was provided by the Real Estate Foundation of British Columbia. Without their support the production of this document would not have been possible. We also take this occasion to thank the Real Estate Foundation of BC for their leadership in promoting a more sustainable region, and for their many years of support to help advance this goal.

Funding to produce this document was also provided by the Landscape Architecture Canada foundation, to whom we also express our deep gratitude.

Sustainability *by* Design

A VISION FOR A REGION OF 4 MILLION

A project of
the Design Centre for Sustainability
at The University of British Columbia

Executive Partners

 Fraser Basin Council

 Sustainable Cities

 Greater Vancouver Regional District

Funding Partners

 THE REAL ESTATE FOUNDATION OF BRITISH COLUMBIA

 VANCOUVER FOUNDATION

 Transports Canada / Transport Canada

 Greater Vancouver Regional District

 LANDSCAPE ARCHITECTURE CANADA FOUNDATION FONDATION D'ARCHITECTURE DE PAYSAGE DU CANADA

 Western Economic Diversification Canada / Diversification de l'économie de l'Ouest Canada

 THE UNIVERSITY OF BRITISH COLUMBIA

Published by the Design Centre for Sustainability
at The University of British Columbia

Room 394 - 2357 Main Mall
Vancouver, British Columbia
Canada V6T 1Z4

Tel: +1(604)822-5148
Fax: +1(604)822-2184
www.dcs.sala.ubc.ca

Written by Patrick Condon, Susan Milley,
Ray Straatsma, Jackie Teed, and Jone Belausteguigoitia
Designed by Jone Belausteguigoitia and Sara Fryer
Edited by Patrick Condon and Jackie Teed
Printed and bound in Canada by 3S Printers Inc.
Distributed by New Society Publishers
PO Box 189, Gabriola Island, BC, Canada
V0R 1X0

Based on research and work resulting from the first year of the project
Sustainability by Design, 2006
www.sxd.sala.ubc.ca

Condon, Patrick M. and Teed, Jackie Editors
Sustainability by Design: A Vision for a Region of 4 Million

Includes bibliographical references
ISBN: 978 - 0- 9780966 - 2 - 5
1. City Planning - Environmental Aspects - British Columbia - Greater
Vancouver. 2. Sustainable development - British Columbia - Greater
Vancouver . I. Condon, Patrick M. II. Teed, Jackie. III. The Design Centre
for Sustainability. The University of British Columbia. IV. Title.

Acknowledgements

We acknowledge all those who have participated in the development of this compilation of work from the first year of Sustainability by Design and all initiatives leading up to it. Without their vision, dedication, and valuable time this publication would not have been possible. Special acknowledgement is given to the project's executive partners as well as to the project's funding partners for providing generous funding and advisory support. Executive partners include: the Fraser Basin Council, the Greater Vancouver Regional District, and the International Centre for Sustainable Cities. Funding partners include: the Greater Vancouver Regional District, the Real Estate Foundation of British Columbia, Transport Canada (MOST Program), the University of British Columbia, the Vancouver Foundation, and Western Economic Diversification Canada.

We would also like to thank all those who have collaborated in providing the SxD project with their efforts and expertise. These include: the James Taylor Chair in Landscape and Liveable Environments; Robert Lane, Robert Liberty, and Mark Seasons for introducing the project's building blocks or study areas — Corridors, Edges, and Nodes— in their presentations at the three public forums held in February and March 2006; Urban Futures for the use of their population and demographic research in developing the population scenarios; the municipalities of Burnaby, Delta, and Langley for their involvement in the case study workshops and charrettes; and all the students in the UBC Sustainable Urban Design 2005 fall studio, who provided the first Sustainability by Design vision.

Finally, we would like to thank all the participants in the three case study workshops and charrettes and in the regional design charrette. The involvement of all those participating in the workshops and four-day charrettes was key to the acceptance of the six guiding principles for sustainable communities in the three different study areas of corridor, edge, and node. The contribution of the over 120 participants in the intensive six-hour regional design charrette was crucial for testing the guiding principles and providing a regional — and sustainable — vision for a fifty-year time frame.

Authorship

This publication was produced in a spirit of collaboration and teamwork by members of the Design Centre for Sustainability at the University of British Columbia. Ray Straatsma was project lead, while Jackie Teed coordinated and edited all parts of the book and is primary author of the Corridor and Node Case Study sections. Susan Milley is primary author of the Edge Case Study section, and Jone Belausteguigoitia is primary author of the population and demographic research. Sara Fryer is acknowledged for her creativity in establishing the book's graphic and layout design. The graphics, diagrams, and illustrations were developed by all members of the project team. Finally, Patrick Condon took leadership in establishing the goals, objectives, scope, and graphic language of the project. He is primary author of the Introduction and Region section, and he also edited all drafts produced by the project team.

the site *is to the* region *what the* cell *is to the* body

table of contents

Left:

Bounded by the Coast Mountains to the north and the Strait of Georgia to the west, the Greater Vancouver Regional District (GVRD) is one of the most highly ecologically constrained regions in North America. These assets, along with visionary long-term planning, also make this one of the most liveable places in the world. Our challenge is to sustain this liveability as our population grows to an expected 4 million in fifty years.

Introduction

The Greater Vancouver Region has earned a reputation as one of the world's most liveable places. That achievement is the direct result of our region's natural assets as well as the visionary long-term planning of the previous generation. Our challenge, in this generation, is to transform our liveable region into a sustainable one. But the same pressures that propel other regions to make unsustainable decisions are also at play here. Citizens and policy makers are not always sure how to proceed, how to know for certain whether a solution to a short-term problem will enhance or impede our long-term progress towards becoming a more sustainable region. In the last twenty years, Greater Vancouver has experienced a population growth of nearly 60 percent, from 1.2 million people in 1981 to almost 2 million in 2001. Similar rates of growth are expected for the future, with a resulting doubling of our population to 4 million in only fifty years. How will the region accommodate this growth sustainably? How will housing, jobs, and transportation be designed, delivered, and distributed? And how are we to do this and still have our aggregate contribution to global warming decline, even as our population doubles?

In the document you are holding, the Design Centre for Sustainability (DCS) attempts to answer these questions by drawing a literal picture of what a sustainable region of 4 million might look like. We call this project Sustainability by Design (SxD). The project's operating principle is that sustainable solutions applied at the scale of the neighbourhood, if widely replicated, may be the crucial ingredient for a sustainable region;

for, just as the health of the human body has everything to do with the health of the individual cells that comprise it, so the sustainability of the metropolitan region depends on the sustainability of the individual neighbourhoods from which it is assembled.

The goal of this project is: *to galvanize support for a sustainable Vancouver region — among citizens, elected officials, government staff, the NGO sector, real estate professionals, and the broader population of community advocates.* We seek to satisfy the need for a clear picture, currently absent in the minds of our citizens and decision makers, of what a sustainable region of 4 million might actually look like. Without an image of what it looks like, it is not surprising that citizens and decision makers don't know how to build it. In Sustainability by Design you see the first iteration of a collaboratively produced vision for a sustainable region for 4 million.

How did we determine how best to delineate this vision? With the help of our SxD Advisory Committee and our partners in the Technical Advisory Committee of the GVRD we arrived at a two-track strategy to meet this goal. One track would have us use a charrette methodology to arrive at viable sustainable development strategies that could apply to certain types of district-scale sites (a charrette is a time-limited, multi-stakeholder design workshop facilitated by skilled designers). The solutions generated at the three case study charrettes could be mined for the basic design principles embodied therein — principles that could then be applied to other similar sites across the region. The three types of sites chosen from a host of volunteer communities were: the corridor site (Kingsway, Burnaby, BC), the node site (200th Street nodes, Langley, BC), and the edge site (East Ladner/Delta Civic Centre, Delta, BC). These three charrettes were "stakeholder driven," meaning that citizens and other stakeholders in the various communities made all of the design decisions about the site, including approving the design and planning targets used in the design brief. The results of these three case study charrettes constitute the first part of Sustainability by Design.

The other track had us looking at the entire region, using design rules that had emerged from the case study charrettes and applying them more broadly. To do this efficiently, we employed the resources of the nation's planners, architects, and landscape architects, all of whom were in town during one week in late June of 2006. Nearly 200 professionals spent a furiously intense six hours creating a giant 5,000 scale map of the region. This map showed where each and every one of the 1 million new housing units required to house an additional 2 million residents would be located. This map represents the first regional scale collaboratively produced vision for how the region might look in 2050, when it will be home for 4 million people. Most important, it embodies the collective wisdom of the citizens and stakeholders who participated in the case study design charrettes. It also provides, again for the first time, a clear picture of what the region will look like if we successfully achieve the goals set out in the GVRD's original Liveable Region Strategic

Plan (LRSP) and its heir, the Sustainable Region Initiative (SRI).

We hope and trust that this contribution will help inform the debate in our region — a debate that seems at a critical stage. We owe it to those who came before us to value their commitment to ensuring a liveable region for us, their children. We owe much more to our children: a sustainable region that helps cool our overheating world.

Six guiding principles for sustainable communities

When approaching the problem of designing a region, one is instantly struck with a question: on what basis are we to proceed? In our case we capitalized on a deep, durable, and ongoing public policy debate that resulted in the formulation of a number of first principles. In the Lower Mainland of British Columbia, three public policy debates have been most influential: The BC Commission on Resources and Environment's "CORE Report,"[1] the Growth Strategies Statutes Amendment Act[2] and the Liveable Region Strategic Plan (LRSP)[3]. All three of these works built from each other and provided a lasting consensus that helped guide a decade of land-use decisions. In short, all three supported the protection of green resources, the provision of adequate and affordable housing throughout the region, and the creation of complete communities where housing, jobs, and services are located conveniently enough that options to the car are conceivable. Of these policy debates, only the LRSP was specifically applied to the Vancouver region. In addition to the general goals mentioned, it identified a

constellation of regional town centres, each to be complete and all to be linked by a web of transit connections.

This robust policy base provided the necessary point of departure for our project. Without it, our work would have been merely speculative. Respect for this broad policy base has resulted in our work being a credible depiction of what our region would look like if it were not only built in conformance with the values expressed in those documents but also went a step further to encompass a vision of the sustainable region that adherence to these values might facilitate. With this in mind, we distilled those general principles for a liveable and sustainable region into a useful design format. The six principles at right are the product of this refining and, ultimately, will become the drivers for the resulting sustainable urban designs. In operation, these principles are synergistic and layered. They truly comprise a case in which the whole is greater than the sum of its parts. Using only one principle to guide design may lead to gains in some areas while producing unintended losses in others (for example, saving fish by reducing density will exacerbate transportation problems and lead to fouled air). Thus, the challenge for the participants became one of combining and layering these principles while trying to minimize the occasional conflicts between them. In the end, these principles may be more important than the designs they generate. If these six simple rules could guide our decisions at the neighbourhood and district scale, the region would certainly be better for it.

Notes

1   CORE Report, *Finding a Common Ground: A Shared Vision for Land Use in British Columbia*, Commission on Resources and the Environment, Vancouver, BC, 1994

2   *Growth Strategies Statutes Amendment Act*, Province of British Columbia Legislative Assembly and Minister of Municipal Affairs, Victoria, BC, 1995

3   *Livable Region Strategic Plan, LRSP*, Greater Vancouver Regional District, Burnaby, BC, 1995

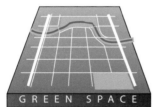
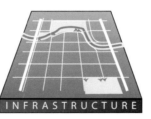

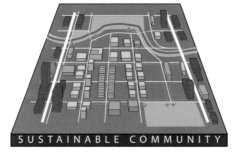

six guiding principles for sustainable communities

1. Good and plentiful **JOBS** close to home.
   Job sites located within communities reduce time spent travelling to work

2. Different **HOUSING** types.
   A range of housing types allows residents of differing economic situations to live in the same neighbourhood and have access to the same services

3. Mixed use **CORRIDORS** accessible to all.
   High density commercial and residential corridors focus growth along transit routes

4. Five minute **WALKING** distance.
   Interconnected street systems link residents with the services they need

5. Access to **NATURAL** areas and parks.
   Green space provides recreation opportunities and connects people with natural systems

6. Lighter, greener, cheaper, smarter **INFRASTRUCTURE**.
   Integrating natural systems reduces infrastructure costs and environmental impact

sustainability by design: a vision for a region of 4 million

Case Study Charrettes

Corridors are linear routes of mobility, connection, access, and community. They have a fundamental role in the spatial organization of both the city and the region. They create essential links for transport, commerce, and other urban functions and connect key urban centres. Corridors also provide an anchor for the identity and vitality of a community, particularly those main streets of commercial and social services that are the "front door" for surrounding neighbourhoods. Well-designed, mixed-use development along major transit corridors revitalizes city neighbourhoods by providing new housing, jobs, and civic and green spaces. When thoughtfully redeveloped, corridors help anchor, rather than divide, the civic life of local communities.

As the population of Greater Vancouver doubles to 4 million over the next fifty years,[1] the region's major corridors, in addition to its town centres, will become increasingly important for accommodating housing and employment. Generally, corridors provide sites where land is relatively inexpensive, transit is easily accessed, and many parcels are ripe for intensification. Over a long period of time, incremental redevelopment along key corridors can evolve with market conditions and proceed without major disruption to surrounding areas. Corridors provide an optimal location for concentrated development.

The Study Site: Kingsway, Burnaby BC
The corridor study site is the portion of Kingsway that lies within the City of Burnaby, between the western border with Vancouver at Boundary Road and the eastern border with New Westminster at 10th Avenue. Kingsway is the site of the original wagon trail route connecting Vancouver with New Westminster along the Kingsway Ridge. It is both a major connector and an emerging collection of

neighbourhoods, linking two Burnaby town centres — Metrotown and Edmonds — and the planned Village Centre of Royal Oak. Kingsway carries commuters and goods between Vancouver, Burnaby, and New Westminster, although this role has declined in recent decades. It also anchors small businesses, light industry, civic facilities, and a major regional shopping district, and it is an important route for residents and workers travelling to and from these amenities. Each of these roles must be recognized in the future development of Kingsway.

The physical character of Kingsway varies along this six-kilometre segment, with more intensive uses along the western portion, a light industrial centre with limited residential use at Royal Oak, and a primarily ground-oriented residential area along Kingsway's eastern segment. Central Park is located at the west end. Town centre intensification and an arterial-model road network have brought increased density and traffic along Kingsway. Many intersecting streets do not connect across Kingsway, and the road network generally lacks a robust grid providing alternative travel routes. Traffic volume increases on the corridor have been mitigated by the SkyTrain line, which parallels Kingsway a few blocks to the south.

A wide, linear ribbon from one-half kilometre north of Kingsway to one kilometre south was examined to include neighbourhood context, including the SkyTrain corridor.

The key outcomes
The crucial question of this case study was this: can a corridor traditionally used as a highway for driving between cities become a walkable and attractive main street for a sustainable urban community? The charrette team answered this question in the affirmative, but making it real will be challenging.

Of the utmost importance is taming Kingsway without unduly diminishing

through-traffic capacity. The proposed street section includes four travel lanes with a single left turn lane and parking on both sides to buffer pedestrians and to provide easy access for patrons. "Neck downs" at all intersections reduce crossing distances to a reasonable maximum of about seventeen metres. Street design speeds are based on a fifty-kilometre per hour travel speed, while intersections and crossing points remain frequent at a maximum separation of 200 metres.

With this basic framework it is possible to redevelop the corridor as an urban avenue serving 30,000 new housing units at the designated town centres of Metrotown and Edmonds, with four-storey mixed-use commercial buildings — ground floor commercial and office or residential above — on portions between. Auto service commercial use remains along Kingsway, reconfigured in a format more compatible with a mixed-use pedestrian environment.

Space for new jobs equal to the number of new households on the corridor was found and incorporated. Key to the strategy is the preservation of the large industrial district in Royal Oak, south of Kingsway. However, the industrial area could also include housing, if that housing were part of a light industrial or business-use building.

Finally, the redevelopment of Kingsway and the adding of billions of dollars worth of new investment provides the capital resources necessary for rebuilding the degraded watersheds below the Kingsway Ridge. New development can be held to a high standard for low impact on receiving watersheds both to the north and the south of the corridor. Development cost charges can be used to finance the reconstruction of street infrastructure, turning grey streets into green ones.

Notes

1   Urban Futures and SxD research

Below:

The corridor study site is the portion of Kingsway within Burnaby, BC. The Kingsway corridor follows the original wagon trail route between Vancouver and New Wesminster. Kingsway is a historic major transportation route between cities. The major challenge for Kingsway is to maintain this transport role while becoming an attractive and walkable "main street" for the community.

50-year
VISION
Corridor

Charrette participants: Ray Allen, Graham Barron, Antonia Beck, Joanne Carne, Paul Cipywnyk, Patrick Condon, Richard Drdul, Sara Fryer, Lee-Anne Garnet, Darlene Gering, Chris Hildred, Kenji Ito, Peeter Liivamagi, Herman Neussler, Stuart Ramsey, Moreno Rossi, Johannes Schuman, Ray Straatsma, Ana Velazquez Martin, Ron Walkey, Robyn Wark, and Ian Wasson.

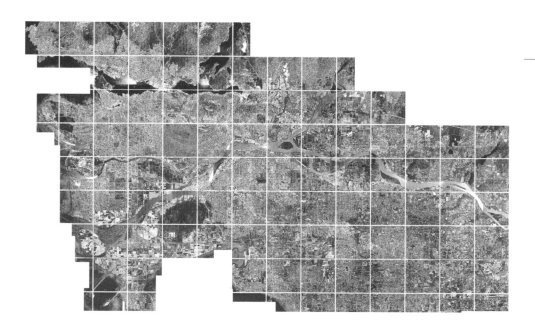

key design targets:

The following fifty-year targets for housing and employment were used to inform design deliberations for the study site. The targets were developed in workshops with city staff and key stakeholders.

- 50,000 - 60,000 new residents;

- 23,000 - 30,000 new housing units;

- 16,000 - 22,000 new jobs;

- 2.1 million – 2.7 million square feet commercial/retail space; and,

- 1.2 million – 1.7 million square feet office and industrial space.

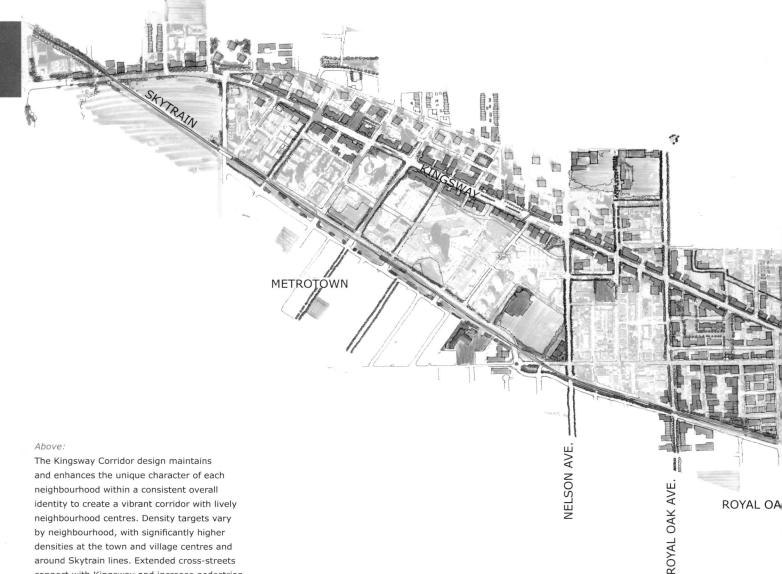

SKYTRAIN

KINGSWAY

METROTOWN

NELSON AVE.

ROYAL OAK AVE.

ROYAL OA

Above:

The Kingsway Corridor design maintains and enhances the unique character of each neighbourhood within a consistent overall identity to create a vibrant corridor with lively neighbourhood centres. Density targets vary by neighbourhood, with significantly higher densities at the town and village centres and around Skytrain lines. Extended cross-streets connect with Kingsway and increase pedestrian and vehicle access between the corridor and surrounding neighbourhoods. An expanded parks network, including the SkyTrain corridor, redeveloped with a parallel recreation and vehicle route links the Kingsway ridge with the surrounding ecological system, and provides a parallel vehicle route to reduce demands on Kingsway.

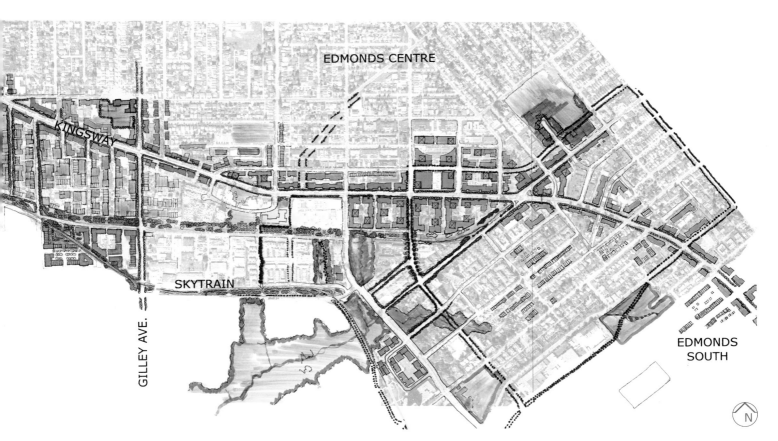

EDMONDS CENTRE

KINGSWAY

SKYTRAIN

GILLEY AVE.

EDMONDS
SOUTH

N

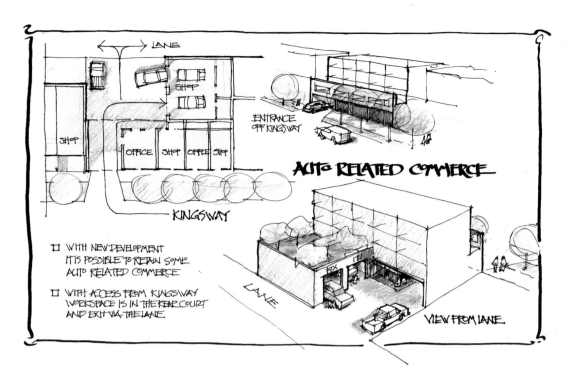

AUTO RELATED COMMERCE

LANE

SHOP

SHOP

OFFICE SHOP OFFICE SHOP

KINGSWAY

ENTRANCE OFF KINGSWAY

□ WITH NEW DEVELOPMENT IT IS POSSIBLE TO RETAIN SOME AUTO RELATED COMMERCE

□ WITH ACCESS FROM KINGSWAY WORKSPACE IS IN THE REAR COURT AND EXIT VIA THE LANE

LANE

FIX

VIEW FROM LANE

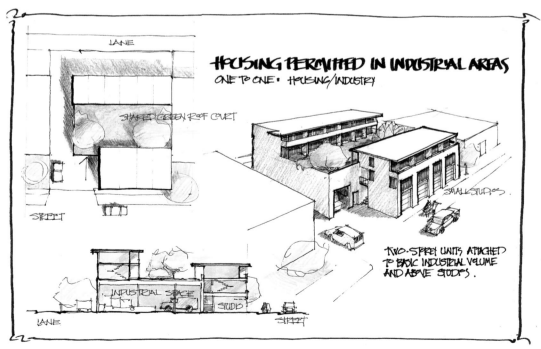

HOUSING PERMITTED IN INDUSTRIAL AREAS
ONE TO ONE : HOUSING/INDUSTRY

LANE

SHARED GREEN ROOF COURT

STREET

SMALL STUDIOS

TWO-STOREY UNITS ATTACHED TO BASIC INDUSTRIAL VOLUME AND ABOVE STUDIOS.

INDUSTRIAL SPACE

STUDIO

LANE

STREET

Kingsway continues to support diverse commercial services along the corridor, particularly in the light industrial area between Royal Oak and Gilley avenues (see below). The continuous façade of street-fronting mixed-use buildings houses shops and offices. The backs of lots, which are accessible by the rear lane, accommodate auto service commercial uses. Driveway access from Kingsway can be maintained, provided that upper storeys of buildings continue over driveways so as to preserve the continuity of the street façade.

Bottom, left:

Light industrial areas along Kingsway provide a good job base for residents and a customer base for nearby services. Newly incorporated live/work studios for artists and craftspeople invigorate these areas and help keep light industrial areas in the city. Innovative housing types include two-storey residential units over existing industrial space or over a studio attached to the sides of buildings. Residents share access to a green roof.

Below:

Significant land areas near Royal Oak Village and between Royal Oak and Gilley avenues are designated for light industrial and commercial uses. Residential uses are also encouraged in these areas, and innovative housing types — such as apartments over light industrial — bring homes close to jobs.

good & plentiful JOBS close to home ©

key charrette conclusions:
job sites located within communities
reduce time spent travelling to work

- Create a corridor with mixed uses on its entire length;

- Develop a dense urban centre at Metrotown to attract and concentrate office uses; and

- Protect industrial lands at Royal Oak by creating opportunities for expansion and intensification of uses, including innovative housing types.

ROYAL OAK AVE.

GILLEY AVE.

IN SINGLE FAMILY AREAS INFILL HAPPENS SLOWLY
— A COACH HOUSE OFF THE LANE, A DUPLEX

INCREMENTAL INFILL

ASSURING SUN PENETRATION

- EQUINOX SUN ANGLE LIMITS BUILDING HEIGHT
- TO ALLOW COMPATIBLE SCALE, SINGLE LOT, MULTI FAMILY BUILDOUT IS ALLOWED

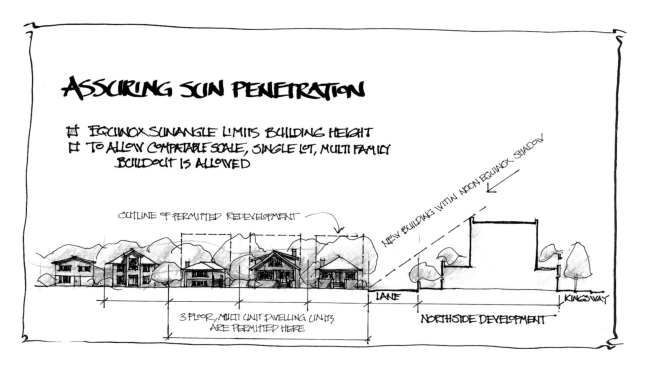

OUTLINE OF PERMITTED REDEVELOPMENT

NEW BUILDING WITHIN NOON EQUINOX SHADOW

3 FLOOR, MULTI UNIT DWELLING UNITS ARE PERMITTED HERE

LANE

KINGSWAY

NORTHSIDE DEVELOPMENT

Top, left:

Incremental infill strategies, such as the addition of coach houses and duplexes, mean that densification occurs gradually, without disrupting existing traditional single-family neighbourhoods along Kingsway.

Bottom, left:

Three-storey, multifamily units located immediately adjacent to Kingsway create a transition to lower-density neighbourhoods. The mixed-use, multifamily buildings along Kingsway step front and back to ensure sunlight penetration for all residents.

Below:

Incorporating residential units into traditionally non-residential areas revitalizes these neighbourhoods and makes them safer at night. In industrial areas such as Royal Oak, the design team allocated an additional 60 percent of floor area to the existing permitted industrial floor area in order to develop residential units on each lot. Built adjacent to or on top of industry, the units share roof-top green space and are ideal for live/work.

different
HOUSING
types

key charrette conclusions:
a range of **housing types** allows residents of differing economic situations to live in the same neighbourhood and to have access to the same services

- Locate higher-density, street-fronting development along Kingsway, with modulated building façades, new public plazas, buildings, and uses;

- Allow up to eight-storey buildings within town centres (Metrotown and Edmonds) and up to four-storey buildings within village areas (Royal Oak);

- Design built form to provide mixed-use commercial and residential occupancies; and

- Situate at least 23,000 new residential units within the Kingsway corridor over the next thirty to fifty years.

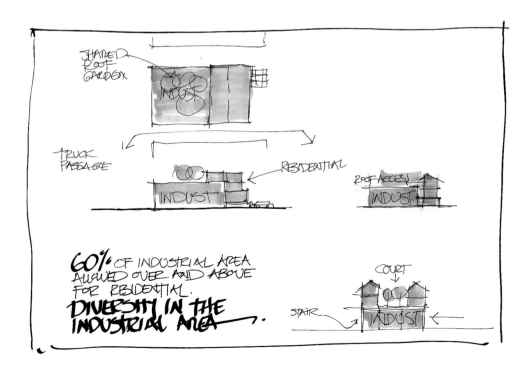

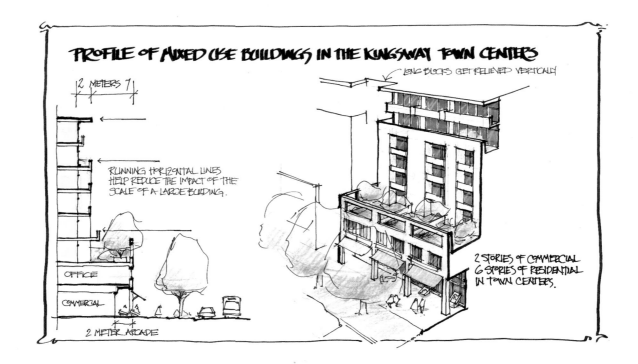

PROFILE OF MIXED-USE BUILDINGS IN THE KINGSWAY TOWN CENTERS

2 METERS

LONG BLOCKS GET RELIEVED VERTICALLY

RUNNING HORIZONTAL LINES HELP REDUCE THE IMPACT OF THE SCALE OF A LARGE BUILDING.

OFFICE

COMMERCIAL

2 METER ARCADE

2 STORIES OF COMMERCIAL
6 STORIES OF RESIDENTIAL
IN TOWN CENTERS.

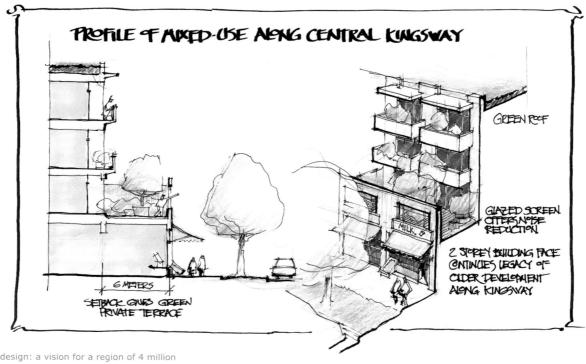

PROFILE OF MIXED-USE ALONG CENTRAL KINGSWAY

GREEN ROOF

GLAZED SCREEN OFFERS NOISE REDUCTION.

MILK

2 STOREY BUILDING FACE CONTINUES LEGACY OF OLDER DEVELOPMENT ALONG KINGSWAY

6 METERS

SETBACK GIVES GREEN PRIVATE TERRACE

Top, left:

Buildings are close to the street to create a continuous, pedestrian-scale street façade. Density targets vary between neighbourhoods, with a corresponding variety of building heights. Metrotown and Edmonds Centre include buildings of six to eight storeys, with two storeys of commercial and office below residential units. Building façades step back at the top to reduce visual impact.

Bottom, left:

Outside of town centres — such as in Royal Oak and Edmonds East — street-front buildings are two to four storeys, with only ground-floor businesses. Building façades step back at two storeys to match the form of older development along Kingsway.

Below:

The Kingsway cross-section accommodates pedestrians, cyclists, transit passengers, and drivers. Narrowed travel lanes — still wide enough to permit goods movement along Kingsway — free up room for dedicated bike lanes and wider sidewalks. Pedestrian-scale, street-oriented buildings with street-level businesses, street trees, and shop canopies all contribute to creating a safe and attractive pedestrian environment. Residences, jobs, services, and parks located along the length of Kingsway provide multiple destinations along the corridor.

mixed use CORRIDORS accessible to all Ⓒ

key charrette conclusions:
high density commercial and residential **corridors** focus growth along transit routes

- Create a multimodal transportation corridor for transit, pedestrians, and cyclists as well as cars;

- Design a walkable, liveable urban street with special attractions and public places; and

- Improve connectivity and route choice on surrounding road and pedestrian networks.

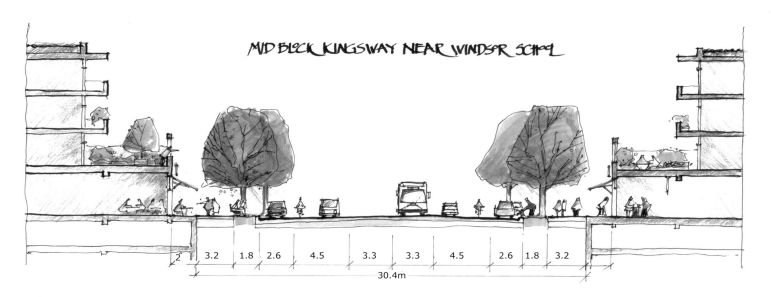

MID BLOCK KINGSWAY NEAR WINDSOR SCHOOL

2 | 3.2 | 1.8 | 2.6 | 4.5 | 3.3 | 3.3 | 4.5 | 2.6 | 1.8 | 3.2

30.4m

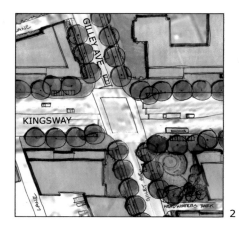

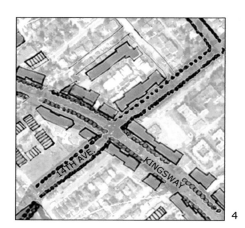

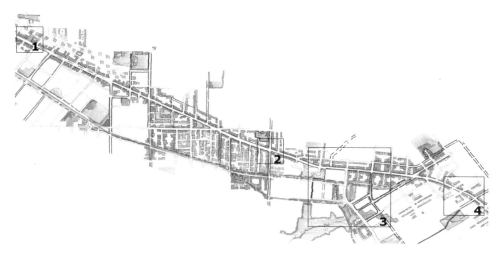

Top, left:

In certain key locations, the charrette team proposes inserting pocket parks into the Kingsway streetscape. Locations where a through-block connection is desired are ideal for such an intervention, which provides an urban oasis.

Top, right:

Buildings are set back from obtuse-angle intersections to provide regular green "living rooms" along Kingsway. Artfully designed public squares front prominent community buildings and other high-visibility locations.

Bottom, left:

Riparian and trail greenway corridors connect Kingsway to adjacent habitat and open space at Deer Lake and the South Slope Ravines. The greenways collect, filter, and infiltrate stormwater and link residents with their natural environment.

Bottom, right:

New street trees line Kingsway and other neighbourhood collector streets, creating a continuous, shaded walking route that contributes to pedestrian scale, reduces the heat island effect, and promotes alternative modes of transportation.

Below:

Connectivity for pedestrians, bikes, and vehicles is improved by repairing the fine grained grid of streets. Streets that formerly stopped short now connect through to Kingsway. New streets break up large contiguous blocks — such as those found between Kingsway, Mackay, Nelson, and cross-streets — creating connectivity and new land parcels to stimulate development.

five
minute
WALKING
distance

key charrette conclusions:
interconnected street systems link
residents with the services they need

- Ensure a consistent, higher-intensity urban quality along Kingsway;

- Develop a unique character and identity for key neighbourhood segments;

- Design enhanced pedestrian qualities and greater connectivity to neighbouring areas; and

- Include a full complement of basic services (schools, shopping, transit) accessible to all at each part of the corridor.

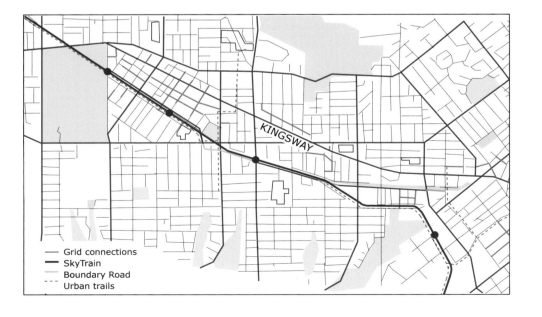

KINGSWAY

— Grid connections
━ SkyTrain
┄ Boundary Road
┈ Urban trails

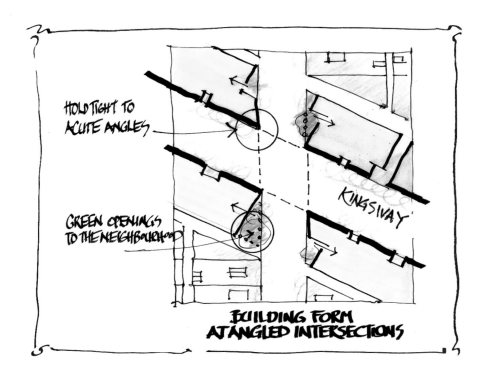

HOLD TIGHT TO
ACUTE ANGLES

GREEN OPENINGS
TO THE NEIGHBOURHOOD

KINGSWAY

**BUILDING FORM
AT ANGLED INTERSECTIONS**

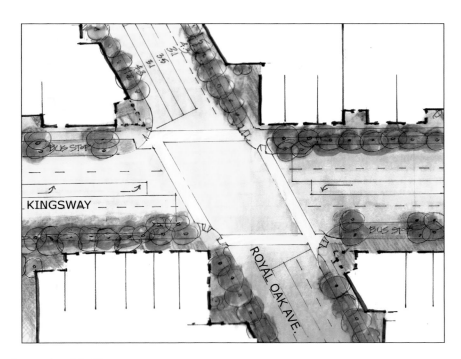

BUS STOP

KINGSWAY

BUS STOP

ROYAL OAK AVE.

Top, left:

The charrette team carefully oriented new buildings along Kingsway to create pocket parks. Kingsway's alignment cuts across the surrounding street grid, forming many angled intersections. New buildings at these intersections fit closely to acute corners but remain square at obtuse corners, thereby creating public space openings in the otherwise continuous street façade.

Bottom, left:

The small, outdoor "green living rooms" at angled intersections — in combination with larger public squares found along Kingsway — contribute to a compelling vista along the street.

Below:

New connections between the corridor and surrounding open space amenities link Kingsway to a broader recreation network of riparian areas, parks, and greenways. The SkyTrain corridor provides a unique opportunity for a feature linear park along the Kingsway Ridge. Artificial streams for storm water, riparian plantings, paths, and lighting invigorate the corridor and create an attractive, comfortable, and safe urban open space for pedestrians and cyclists.

key charrette conclusions:
green spaces provide recreation opportunities and connect people with **natural systems**

- Celebrate the Kingsway Ridge by connecting and integrating new and existing green spaces on the ridge to stream and riparian areas to the north and south;

- Provide new parks within 500 metres' walking distance of every citizen;

- Create a green street network featuring trees and planted boulevards for ecological services, transit stops, and public gathering spaces; and

- Upgrade and improve existing green spaces to create attractive, usable public spaces.

Before   *After*

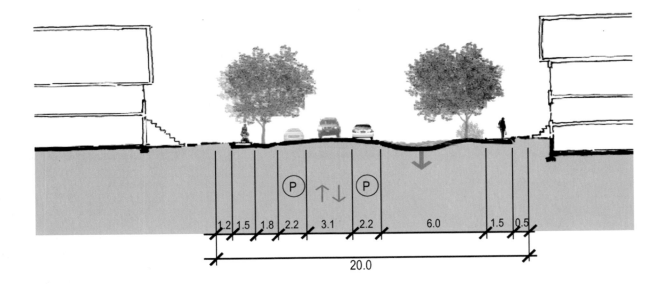

1.2 1.5 1.8 2.2 3.1 2.2 6.0 1.5 0.5

20.0

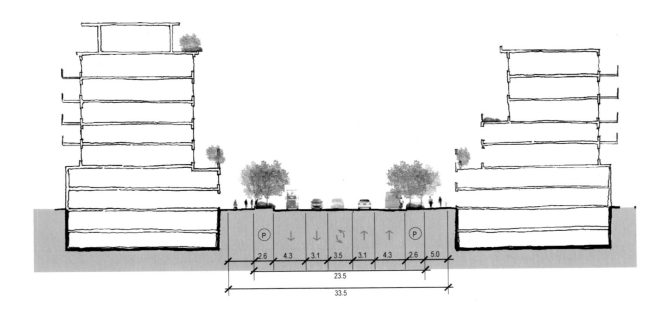

2.6 4.3 3.1 3.5 3.1 4.3 2.6 5.0

23.5

33.5

Top, left:

Kingsway's infrastructure supports a restored urban watershed ecology. A roadside swale collects and naturally filters stormwater along residential streets as it infiltrates to recharge groundwater.

Bottom, left:

Raingardens that collect and filter storm water for infiltration alternate with parking lots along local collector streets. Porous asphalt and concrete on roads and sidewalks, raingardens in traffic bulges, green roofs, and parks and open spaces designed for infiltration also contribute to increased site permeability.

Below:

As well as providing recreational functions, the riparian areas, parks and greenways surrounding Kingsway corridor are ecologically significant. Storm water infiltration along the ridge-top corridor and surrounding neighbourhoods eventually feeds into both Deer Lake (to the north), and the South Slope Ravines (to the south) and helps restore their ecological function. New parks and green corridors reinforce the connection between Kingsway and these riparian areas and highlight their importance to the community.

lighter, greener, cheaper, smarter
INFRASTRUCTURE ©

key charrette conclusions:
integrating natural systems reduces **infrastructure** costs and environmental impact.

- Provide rainwater and stormwater treatment for parks, open spaces, and streets, including swales in centre medians, rain gardens at curb bulges, and porous asphalt and concrete;

- Integrate green roofs, water infiltration and detention, and greywater recycling into new developments, as part of a comprehensive green infrastructure network; and,

- Use green buildings to reduce energy loads.

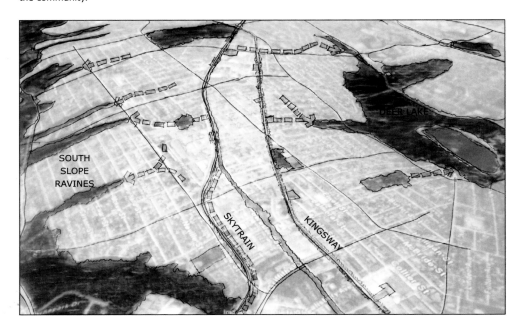

DEER LAKE

SOUTH SLOPE RAVINES

SKYTRAIN

KINGSWAY

Edges are the spaces adjoining two different land uses. Some edges are integrative spaces that create a seam between abutting land uses, while others function as dividing lines or merely taper off. The two types of edge under examination here are (1) the contentious edge between rural and urban land uses and (2) the edge formed by major roads passing through a community.

The rural/urban edge is particularly complex. In practice, Agricultural Land Reserve (ALR) zoning requirements define these edges politically, while hedgerow and fence buffers set them apart physically. Yet, while these edges segregate urban and agricultural land uses, historically they have not prevented the gradual exclusion of agricultural land from encroachment. Sensitively designed integrative edges can better protect agricultural land. As dedicated public spaces, integrative edges increase community familiarity with agriculture and cultivate understanding and community stewardship. Dedicated public edges also provide permanent containment to development, contributing to food security and sustainability throughout the region.

The Study Site:
East Ladner, the Corporation of Delta, BC
The edge study site includes 576 hectares (1,425 acres), encompassing East Ladner plus some adjacent lands. Agricultural land surrounds Ladner, and the study site includes rural parcels. Urban/rural edges are located to the south and east of the study site. These are typical segregating edges intended to prevent physical access, and they create an abrupt separation between land uses with homes backing onto the edge.

Highway 17 and Ladner Trunk Road (Highway 10) create strong physical barriers within the community, particularly between East Ladner and the Delta Civic Centre. Both roads are currently classed as provincial highways, providing major commuter and goods movement as well as port and ferry access. The proposed South Fraser Perimeter Road[1] will reduce the current high traffic volumes, allowing the current Highway 17 to function more as a local arterial road. The corridor design must create an integrative edge that reconnects the community and incorporates the needs of drivers and pedestrians.

The study site includes the Delta Civic Centre, which should be the civic and employment heart of East Ladner. However, the centre lacks a sense of place and is segregated from the community by Highway 17 and Ladner Trunk Road.

The key outcomes
Turning barriers into seams and both connecting and protecting agricultural lands were the two challenges for this design team. For the urban/rural edge, the foremost aim is to protect agricultural land from encroaching development without building a barrier. The proposed thick greenway edge connects the community with a continuous, multimodal path, incorporates allotment gardens, and provides biodiversity and habitat for birds and other wildlife. As a park, the edge is dedicated public space that cannot be developed in perpetuity. Well-designed public edges also increase adjacent property values, which can contribute to edge mitigation funds. In specific locations, controlled higher-density development at the edge is proposed to fund adjacent land improvement and publicly accessible agricultural operations.

New commercial, mixed-use, and institutional infill supported by new pedestrian and vehicle connections to the surrounding community incorporate jobs and housing into the Civic Centre. A new theatre and museum reinforce the public nature of the centre, which also becomes the green community heart, where additional open space collects, cleans, and infiltrates stormwater.

Residential development close to the street civilizes Ladner Trunk Road and Highway 17. The proposed Highway 17 section includes two (as opposed to the original four) travel lanes in each direction, leaving room for a sidewalk on one side and a multimodal greenway on the other. Dedicated at-grade crossings replace the current overpass and bring pedestrians back to the street. Mixed-use buildings at the four corners of the highways' intersection mark this as the centre of the new community.

Notes

1   At the time of the charrette, the precise location of the South Fraser Perimeter Road had not yet been determined.

The edge study site includes 576 hectares (1,425 acres) and encompasses East Ladner as well as additional lands bounded by: Crescent Slough to the north, 72nd Street to the east, the former BC Rail right-of-way to the south, and 57th Street to the west. Agricultural lands surround the community of Ladner, and the study site includes private and public, currently farmed, and vacant parcels. Urban/ rural edges are located to the south and east of the study site. Highway 17 and Ladner Trunk Road also create edges, dividing East Ladner and the Delta Civic Centre from the rest of the community.

50-year VISION Edge   Ⓔ

Charrette participants: Jeff Barker, Jone Belausteguigoitia, Robert Butler, Roger Emsleys, Deana Grinnell, Kelly Guichon, Gary Haylow, Sara Howie, Lin Ji, Lisa King, Thomas Leathem, Nancy McLean, Markus Merkins, Susan Milley, Linda Neilsen, Teresa O'Reilly, Lisa Parker, Tony Pellett, Mark Pickersgill, Edward Porter, Marcy Sangret, Howard Smid, Karen Thomas, Bob Worden, Alan Wawyk, Hon Yee, and Kathleen Zimmerman.

key design targets:

The following fifty-year targets for housing and employment were used to inform design deliberations for the study site. The targets were developed through workshops with city staff and key stakeholders.

- 1,900 to 2,100 new residents;

- 850 to 950 new housing units;

- 1,620 to 1,650 new jobs; and

- 57,000 to 63,000 square feet of commercial/retail space.

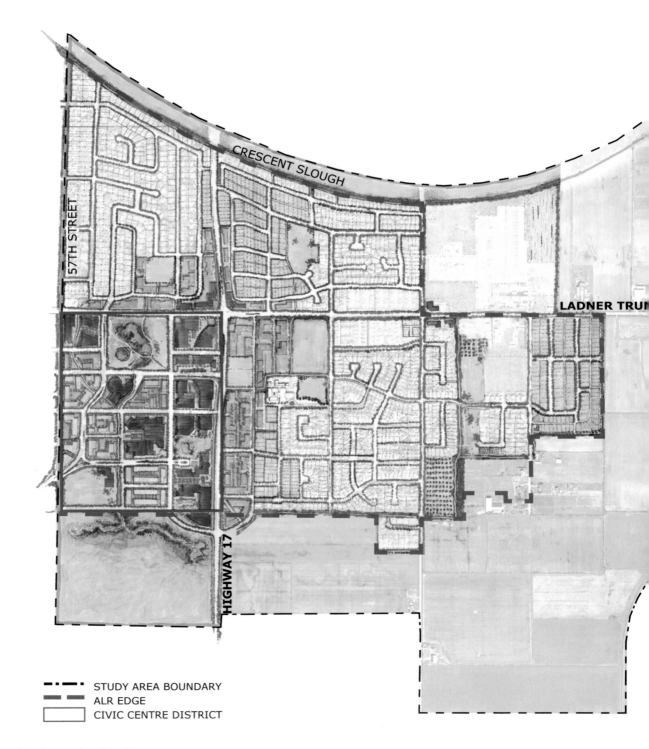

CRESCENT SLOUGH

57TH STREET

LADNER TRU

HIGHWAY 17

—·—· STUDY AREA BOUNDARY
— — — ALR EDGE
☐ CIVIC CENTRE DISTRICT

Left:

The proposed design creates a vibrant community heart at the Civic Centre, with residential, commercial, and institutional infill supported by new significant pedestrian and vehicle connections to the surrounding community. Surrounding residential neighbourhoods remain, and gradual infill of mixed-use, ground oriented, and medium-density residential development provides diverse future housing options. Throughout the site, a reconnected grid of streets provides access to neighbourhoods.

Mixed-use buildings at the intersection of Highway 17 and Ladner Trunk Road mark the new centre of East Ladner and the entryway to Ladner proper. Buildings on both roads are close to the street. The narrower Highway 17 section includes two travel lanes in each direction, leaving room for sidewalks and street trees. At-grade crossings replacing the existing overpass reintegrate pedestrians into the street.

A continuous multimodal greenway creates a thick, continuous public edge between urban and rural uses. A shared desire to retain agricultural land for posterity by embedding it within a collective community consciousness of value, pride, and shared responsibility leads to this and other edge strategies.

key charrette conclusions:
jobs sites located within communities
reduce time spent travelling to work

- Revitalize the Civic Centre by integrating existing uses with new commercial, mixed-use, and institutional uses that bring employment opportunities;

- Establish the Civic Centre as the cultural heart of the community, which will be attractive to many businesses and events; and

- Encourage home-based businesses within the Civic Centre and throughout the community to provide employment diversity.

Left:
The Delta Civic Centre complements Ladner's existing historic centre as a vibrant community and employment "heart." The charrette team proposed that the centre be Ladner's cultural hub, with a new theatre, museum, and open spaces linked by strong pedestrian and vehicle connections to transit and the surrounding community. Currently underutilized spaces, including the former racetrack, will gradually accommodate new and expanded buildings to create more closely knit, interrelated parcels. Commercial, mixed-use, and institutional infill creates job opportunities for all residents. Home-based businesses located throughout the centre in above-garage offices with rear-lane access also support employment diversity.

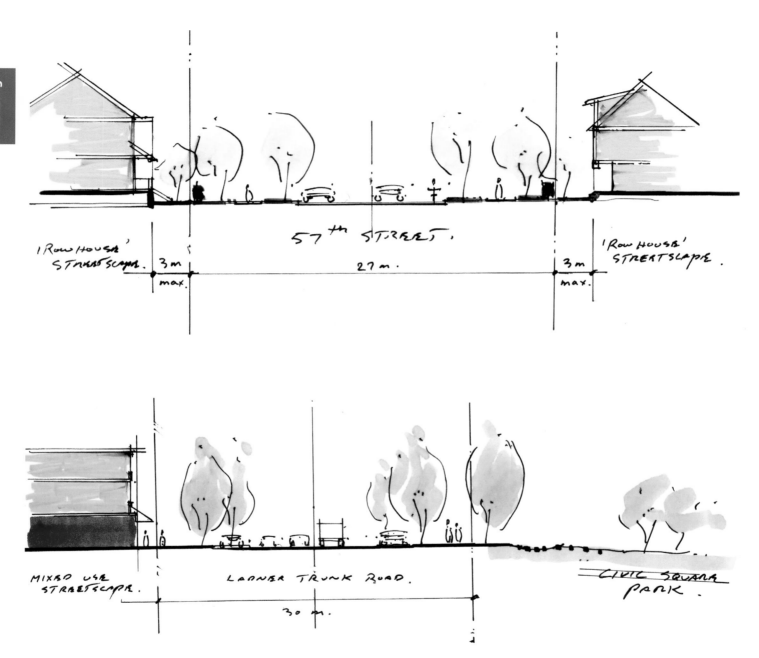

'RowHouse'
STREETSCAPE.   3m
                     max.   57th STREET.
                                                        27m.   3m   'RowHouse'
                                                                                               max.   STREETSCAPE.

MIXED USE
STREETSCAPE.   LARNER TRUNK ROAD.   CIVIC SQUARE
                                        30m.   PARK.

key charrette conclusions:
a range of **housing types** allows residents
of differing economic situations to live
in the same neighbourhood and to have
access to the same services

- Locate new mixed-use apartments (200
uph) and ground-oriented and medium-
density residential (90-100 uph) in the
Civic Centre and along Highway 17 to
ensure proximity to jobs and transit and
to create vibrant, safe, and well-used
spaces; and

- Redevelop certain existing single-family
lots into townhouse units or subdivide
with carriage houses and rear-lane
access to promote housing affordability
and choice.

Top left:

The study site has diverse housing types throughout.
Higher-density street-front row housing around the
Civic Centre, particularly along collector streets,
provides affordable living options and smaller homes
suited to seniors or assisted living situations in
close proximity to services. Throughout the study
area, carriage homes and subdivided single-family
lots accessed by new rear lanes provide increased
housing options.

Bottom left:

The highest-density residential uses are located
along Ladner Trunk Road, where three- to four-
storey mixed-use buildings with residential units
above ground level commercial contribute to housing
diversity and enhance the pedestrian experience on
the street. Higher-density housing and commercial
uses around the civic precinct contribute to a lively
Civic Centre.

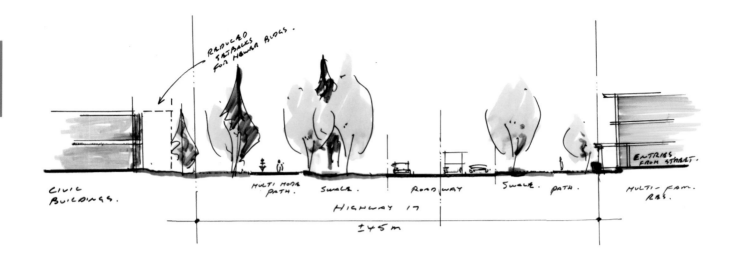

REDUCED SETBACKS FOR HIGHER BLDGS.

ENTRIES FROM STREET.

CIVIC BUILDINGS.   MULTI MODE PATH.   SWALE.   ROADWAY   SWALE.   PATH.   MULTI-FAM. RES.

HIGHWAY 17

±45m

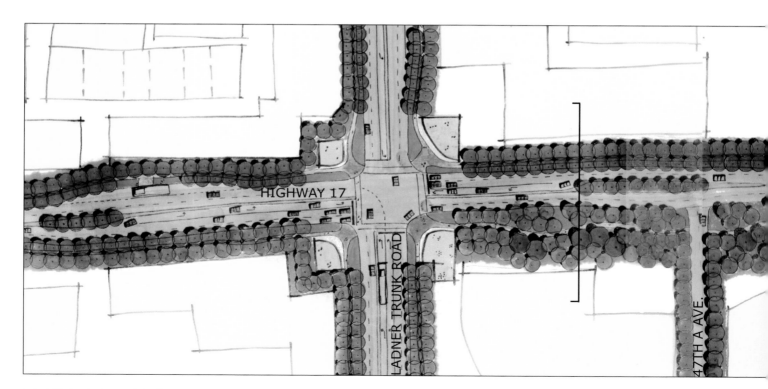

HIGHWAY 17

LADNER TRUNK ROAD

47TH A AVE.

Top, left:

The reduced Highway 17 section includes two travel lanes in each direction, leaving room for wide "greenway boulevards" on both sides. On the east side, ground-oriented, multifamily housing has vehicle access from rear streets or lanes and street-front pedestrian access from a new two-metre-wide sidewalk. On the west side, new civic buildings have reduced setbacks to bring buildings closer to the multimodal greenway. Swales on both sides of the street collect, filter, and infiltrate stormwater, turning grey streets green.

Below:

Mixed-use buildings frame the intersection of Highway 17 and Ladner Trunk Road to create a distinct and identifiable entryway to Ladner. At-grade crossings to the civic heart replace the current pedestrian overpasses, and on-street bus stops replace the former bus loop, improving transit accessibility for residents and commuters and bringing pedestrians back to the street. Ladner Trunk Road and other collector streets continue to function as primary farm vehicle routes.

mixed use
CORRIDORS
accessible to all

key charrette conclusions:
high density commercial and residential **corridors** focus growth along transit routes

- Transform Highway 17 into a local street with fewer lanes, street-fronting mixed-use development, transit access, and ample "greenway boulevards";

- Define a mixed-use and pedestrian-oriented entryway into the community; and

- Preserve key rural corridors to ensure connectivity for the farming community throughout East Ladner.

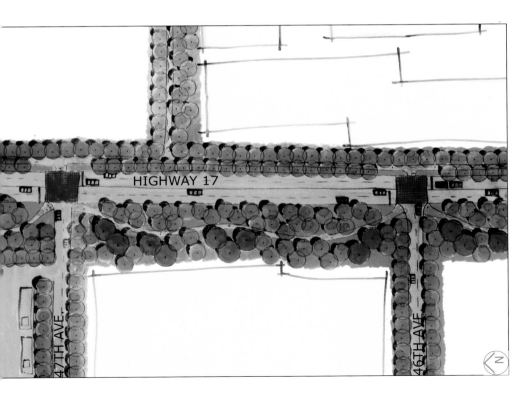

Left:

Bringing residents within walking distance of agriculture connects people to food systems and fosters a shared sense of community between urban and rural residents. A controlled, higher density development pocket at Highway 17 and the ALR boundary creates a connection between adjacent compact neighbourhoods and agricultural land, and links into a multimodal greenway network. Developing a small portion of this agricultural parcel directly funds the reclamation and improvement of the remainder for use as a lower-intensity, publicly-accessible agricultural operation. This type of scheme is only appropriate where agricultural land cannot be revitalized through typical means, and where the sale of farmland at market prices for these explicitly agri-urban uses will benefit both farmer and developer.

Below:

Throughout the community, a gradual shift from a disconnected, cul-de-sac street pattern to an interconnected grid significantly improves accessibility and way-finding. The new hierarchical street system disperses traffic to reduce volumes on arterials, making them more pedestrian friendly. Interconnected streets also provide a continuous, tree-lined pedestrian and bicycle network. New rear lanes provide additional walking and biking routes.

five
minute
WALKING
distance

key charrette conclusions:
interconnected street systems link
residents with the services they need

- Develop a multimodal greenway network linked to significant places, parks and transit;

- Bring people within walking distance of publicly accessible agriculture to connect urban and rural residents and create a shared sense of community; and,

- Transform cul-de-sacs into a connected grid of streets to encourage walkability and multimodal transportation.

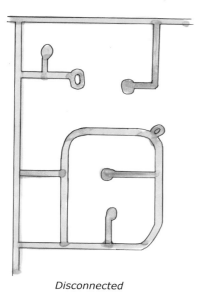

Disconnected

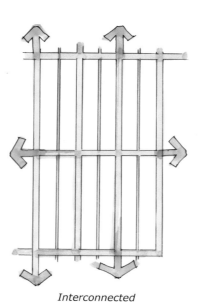

Interconnected

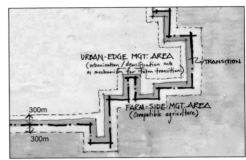

URBAN-EDGE MGT. AREA
(urbanization/densification acts
as mechanism for farm transition)

TRANSITION

FARM-SIDE MGT. AREA
(compatible agriculture)

300m

300m

Res.

Multi modal greenway

Ditch

Large lot Ag.

Bottom and top left, facing page:

Along the urban/rural edge, a continuous multi-modal greenway provides a thick and permanent edge to protect and integrate agricultural land. The greenway incorporates allotment gardens and provides biodiversity and habitat for wildlife. It connects the community and provides a source of recreation, education, and stewardship. A densely planted ditch is a physical barrier but not a solid visual barrier between urban and agricultural uses. Rather than turning their backs, houses front toward agriculture to take advantage of rural vistas.

Top right, facing page:

Houses near parks experience increased market value, which here contributes to an edge-mitigation fund. Development within a 300 metre wide "urban edge-management area" contributes to the fund, which facilitates development of compatible uses within the abutting 300 metre wide "agricultural edge-management area." The multimodal greenway is located within the first 30-50 metres of the urban edge to provide additional transition between uses.

Below:

Thick edges protect agriculture and invite stewardship of agricultural production. Stewardship opportunities include smaller agricultural productions, collective farming, and urban edge allotments that increase community participation. Market gardens and local food markets also respond to escalating market interest in organic, local foods. Many of these activities can take place in the urban/agricultural edge.

access to
NATURAL
areas & parks

key charrette conclusions :
green spaces provide recreation opportunities and connect people with **natural systems**

- Develop a thick, multimodal greenway edge to protect agricultural land from encroachment and connect urban and rural residents to each other and key destinations throughout the community;

- Design multimodal greenways to support habitat and stormwater management; and,

- Use development within a 300 metre wide "urban edge-management area" to fund compatible uses within the abutting 300 metre "agricultural edge-management area".

Before

After

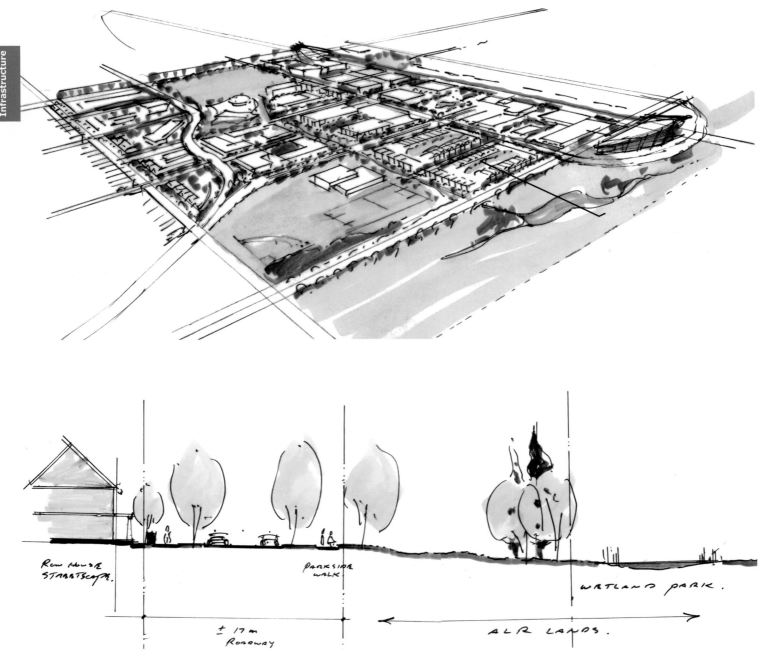

ROW HOUSE
STREETSCAPE.

PARKSIDE
WALK

WETLAND PARK.

± 17 m
ROADWAY

ALR LANDS.

Top and bottom, left:

The charrette team envisioned the Civic Centre as the "green heart" of the community. Given Delta's high water table, the team incorporated water management into all new and retrofit developments. New open space brackets the centre, with a storm water retention pond at the north edge linked to a larger wetland-habitat at the south end via a stream greenway. This green infrastructure system collects, filters, and infiltrates storm water. A geothermal system heats and cools the institutional, civic, and commercial buildings, as well as the medium density residential in and around the centre. All new and retrofitted buildings feature green roofs . Street trees throughout the community provide habitat, shade and rainwater mitigation, and create a pedestrian scale.

Below:

The Civic Centre stormwater system links to new and existing irrigation ditches throughout the community. Swales or pervious paving are also a feature in community greenways, which connect to the centre or other existing and new parks.

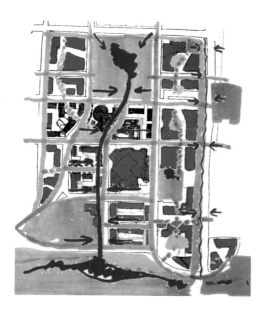

lighter, greener, cheaper, smarter
INFRASTRUCTURE ⓔ

key charrette conclusions:
integrating natural systems reduces **infrastructure** costs and environmental impact

- Plant street trees throughout the community for rainwater absorption and CO_2 sequestration in order to reduce energy use by decreasing the heat island effect and to decrease vehicle use by providing attractive, shaded, pedestrian-scale streets;

- Require green buildings, roofs, and greywater recycling for all new and retrofitted buildings in the Civic Centre; and

- Develop a district geothermal system to heat and cool all civic, institutional, commercial, and medium-density residential areas in and around the Civic Centre.

Nodes are points of dense land use connected to each other and to surrounding residential neighbourhoods by important community corridors. Nodes are complete communities, each including residential, business/commercial, recreation, and ecological land uses. They evolve with different overall densities and characters over time, but the five-minute walking distance generally defines a node's size, with density decreasing with increased distance from the centre. In a well-designed community the edges of nodes overlap, placing all residents within a five-minute walk of their daily needs.

Nodes are an important part of the Greater Vancouver Regional District's Liveable Region Strategic Plan, which seeks to achieve a compact metropolitan region by concentrating growth in a number of town centres. Generally, regional and municipal town centres are key locations of major residential and job land uses, with smaller village and neighbourhood town centres accommodating local residents and workers. Over time, within each community many different kinds of nodes develop, which together can provide for all needs.

The Study Site: four nodes on 200th Street, Township of Langley BC

The node study sites are located at key cross-streets along 200th Street in the Township of Langley. This area was first inhabited by the Kwantlen band, which is part of the Sto:lo Nation. European settlement came with the Hudson's Bay Company, which established the Hudson's Bay Farm east of Willoughby, and the local economy continues to be strongly rural-based with other job sources rapidly increasing. The charrette team studied the area within a five-minute walk around each of the node intersections (a circle with a 500-metre radius) as well as a narrower

band of land on either side of 200th Street between the nodes.

Strung along 200th Street, the nodes influence and reflect the character of the corridor. 200th Street is a major north-south commuter and goods transportation route. The township is divided by the Trans-Canada Highway, and 200th Street currently offers the only direct connection between north and south neighbourhoods. 200th Street also provides access to Langley Regional Town Centre, the Canada/United States border, and the Fraser Highway — an important east-west corridor — and will connect with many additional neighbourhoods following the construction of the Golden Ears Bridge. The design of the corridor and the nodes must complement each other in order to incorporate the needs of transportation and residents alike.

Community plans for many of the neighbourhoods making up the nodes give some direction for future development. The northern nodes — 80th and 83rd avenues — are jobs centres and are wrapped by an extensive network of preserved Latimer Creek tributaries. The southernmost node — 64th Avenue — marks the edge between the township and the Langley Regional Town Centre and reinforces that centre's land uses. In between, the 72nd Avenue node is primarily residential. These two southern nodes have the potential for riparian habitat restoration throughout.

Rural heritage is important to the identity of the Township of Langley. The Agricultural Land Reserve protects substantial areas of agricultural land, restricting development to the Urban Development Zone. The township celebrates the proximity of urban and rural land uses by encouraging aesthetic references and physical connectivity between developed areas and the surrounding open spaces.

The key outcomes

This case study addressed a twofold

challenge: to develop a series of nodes that both reflect the distinct character of each neighbourhood and meet the future needs of the community. Because these nodes centre on 200th Street, the charrette team also had to examine how this highway corridor could transform into a walkable and attractive "main street" without overly reducing through-traffic capacity.

One of the charrette team's guiding principles was to preserve the Latimer Creek tributaries and to restore other watercourses. A preserved tributaries and trails network contains and connects the northern nodes and links schools, parks, and other key pedestrian routes with a grand open space system. In southern nodes, a fine-grained network of greenways and canals channels daylighted watercourses and people throughout the neighbourhoods. Overall, this green network creates the connective tissue tying the 200th Street nodes into a community.

The expected lifespan of existing development influences the development pattern of each node. The nodes incorporate over 10,000 new jobs: high-tech and light-industrial in the northern nodes, with tourist commercial at the highway, and boutique shopping at the 64th Street node. All nodes accommodate home-based businesses.

The nodes include over 20,000 new homes. Each node has a mix of all housing types, but each also has a different ratio of these types. Generally, greenways and busier streets have the highest-density residential uses, and only the highest-density nodes have point towers.

Connecting the nodes, 200th Street is a multiway boulevard that accommodates pedestrians, cyclists, rapid transit, commuters, and goods movement within a safe and well-designed street section. Detailed articulation of the street section changes in response to surrounding context, encouraging slower traffic flow so that pedestrian crossings can occur every 200 metres within nodes.

Originally, four locations along 200th Street in the Township of Langley were selected as the node study sites, from south to north: 64th, 72nd, 80th, and 86th avenues. Early design explorations suggested the addition of a fifth node at 83rd Avenue, with the 86th Avenue site revisioned as a community gateway. As the nodes centre on 200th Street, the charrette team had to examine how this highway corridor could transform into a walkable and attractive "main street" without overly reducing through-traffic capacity.

50-year VISION Nodes

Charrette participants: Elaine Anderson, Elizabeth Anderson, Brad Badelt, Warren Byrd, Jason Chu, John Conicella, Paul Cordeiro, Paul Crawford, Farzaneh Ghassemi, Rhys Griffiths, Amy Hennessey, Melissa Johnson, Gary MacKinnon, Patrick Marples, Sarah McMillan, Al Neufeld, Doug Paterson, Ramin Seifi, Nalon Smith, Travis Stasney, Ben Taddei, Jackie Teed and John Turner.

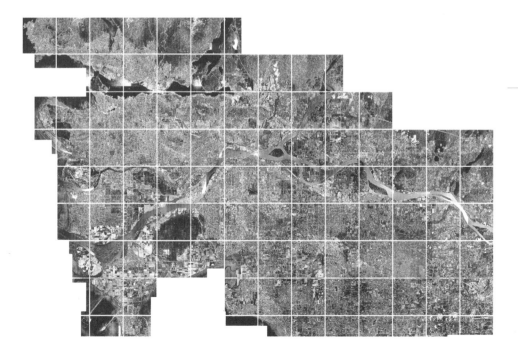

key design targets:

The following fifty-year targets for housing and employment were used to inform design deliberations for the study site. The targets were developed in workshops with city staff and key stakeholders.

- 25,000 to 28,000 residents;

- 13,900 to 20,800 new housing units;

- 8,060 to 10,650 new jobs;

- 930,000 square feet commercial/retail space; and,

- 1.0 to 1.8 million square feet office and industrial space.

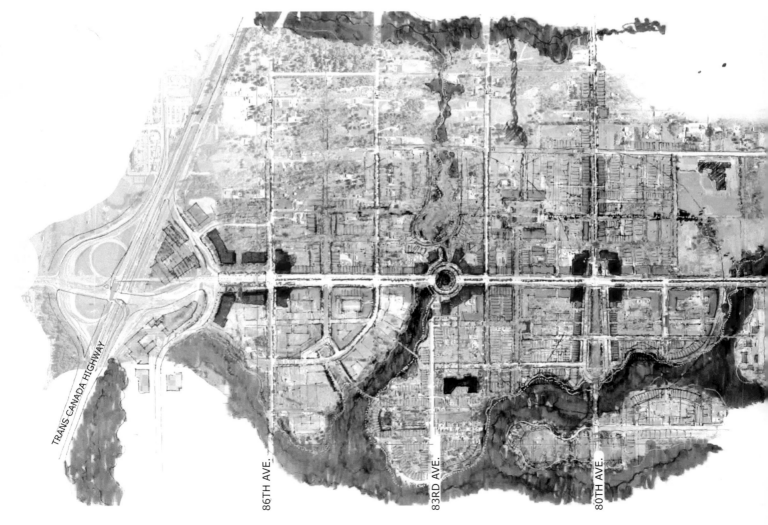

TRANS-CANADA HIGHWAY

86TH AVE.

83RD AVE.

80TH AVE.

Below:

200th Street links four distinctive nodes. In the north, the 83rd Avenue node centres on a roundabout connecting the Latimer Creek corridor across 200th Street to a neighbourhood park in the east. A few blocks south, the 80th Avenue node features a linear urban green linking Latimer Creek to Willoughby Town Centre at 216th Street. These nodes are key business and jobs centres, with high residential densities and contiguous areas of preserved open space.

In the south, the 64th Avenue node creates a commercial and residential edge to Langley Regional Town Centre. The heart of the node shifts south to Willowbrook Drive, the new community shopping street, and centres on a civic plaza proposed to front the new Municipal Hall. This is the highest-density node, with commercial and civic uses and residential point towers. At centre, the 72nd Avenue node is a lower-density residential neighbourhood with a small commercial centre. Mixed-use buildings set back from the west edge of 200th Street create a Market Green, a venue for the community farmers' market. Revitalized creek corridors and many smaller open spaces characterize these nodes.

50-year VISION Nodes

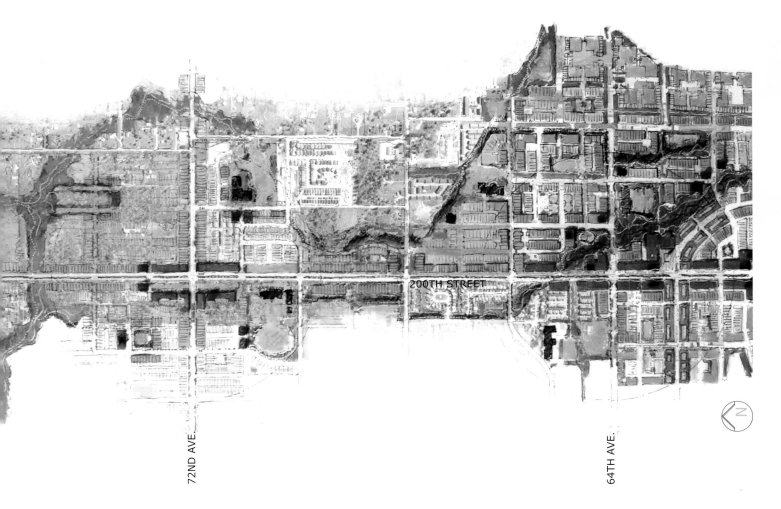

200TH STREET

72ND AVE.

64TH AVE.

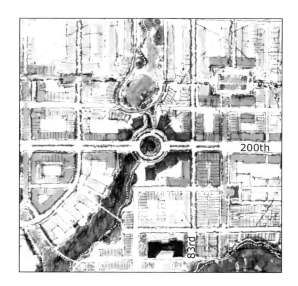

200th

83rd

200th

72nd

Node
Jobs

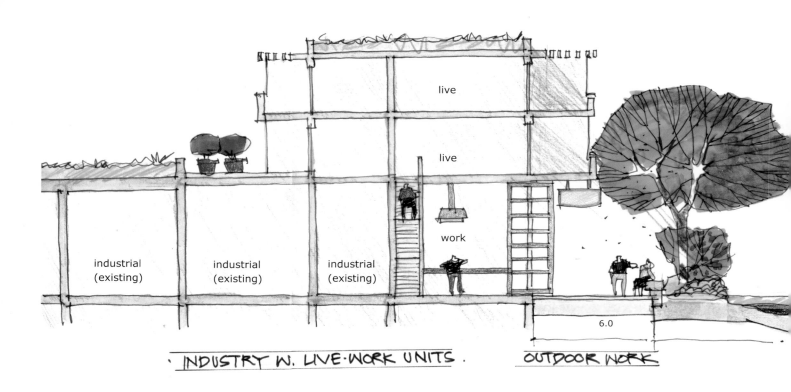

live

live

work

industrial
(existing)

industrial
(existing)

industrial
(existing)

6.0

INDUSTRY W. LIVE·WORK UNITS .   OUTDOOR WORK

Left:

Every node has some jobs, but the 80th, 83rd, and 64th avenue nodes are key job centres. The location, density, and type of jobs help to define a unique character for each node. Light-industrial (light purple) clustered around the north edge of the 83rd Avenue node identifies this neighbourhood as a significant job area. The 72nd Avenue node has some commercial jobs as well as home-based businesses.

Below:

Innovative residential types incorporated into job areas encourage people to live where they work. Retrofitted and new large-scale light-industrial, high-tech, and retail outlets include live-work units. For existing buildings, the new residential unit "barnacles" to the present structure, which is also retrofitted with a green roof.

good & plentiful
JOBS
close to home

key charrette conclusions:
jobs sites located within communities reduce time spent travelling to work

- Locate some jobs at every node, but identify key nodes — such as around 64th and 80th avenues at 200th Street — and locate the majority of jobs there;

- Design innovative housing types to incorporate living into job centres, particularly into business and industrial areas; and

- Use the location, density, and type of jobs to help define the character of each node.

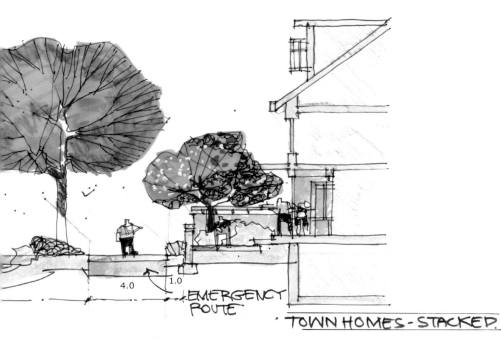

4.0   1.0

EMERGENCY ROUTE

TOWN HOMES - STACKED.

INDUSTRIAL RESIDENTIAL SEPARATION.

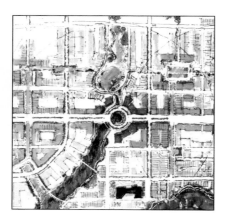

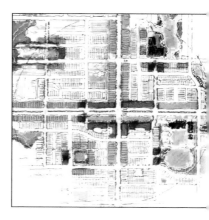

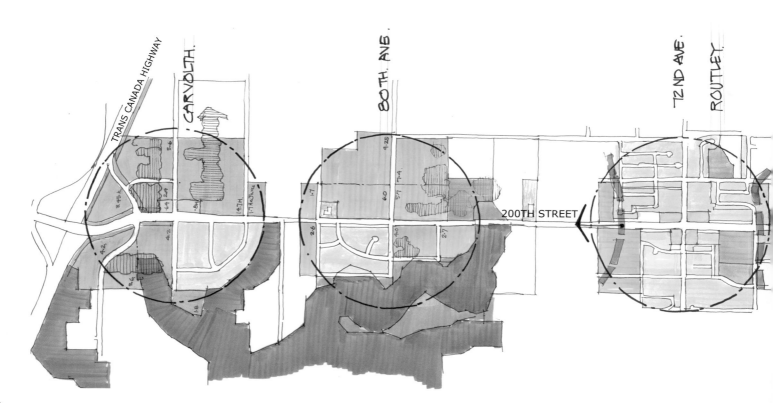

TRANS CANADA HIGHWAY

CARVOLTH.

80TH. AVE.

72 ND. AVE.

ROUTLEY.

200TH STREET

Left, top and bottom:

Each node has a unique mix of existing building stock that influences how rapidly redevelopment occurs. Much of the Carvolth neighbourhood — located just west of the highway — is ready for immediate redevelopment. The 80th, 83rd, and 64th avenue nodes primarily contain lands that will be ready for redevelopment within the next fifteen years. The 72nd Avenue node is generally populated by recently completed residential development, which won't be ready for redevelopment for thirty to forty-five years.

The expected lifespan of existing development also influences the development pattern of each node. The node at 72nd remains as lower-density residential with some neighbourhood commercial. The 80th, 83rd, and 64th avenue nodes incorporate most higher-density residential — including condominiums as well as stacked and ground-oriented townhomes. But every node has at least some of each housing type.

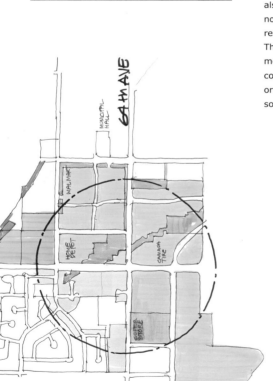

different
HOUSING
types

key charrette conclusions:
a range of **housing types** allows residents of differing economic situations to live in the same neighbourhood and to have access to the same services

- Provide a full range of housing types to suit all income, age, and family needs in every node, but emphasize different housing types between nodes;

- Expect nodes with new building stock — such as 72nd Avenue at 200th Street — to develop slowly, beginning as a small neighbourhood centre at medium to low densities;

- Locate the most high-density rowhouses and apartments in nodes that are considered important commercial and job areas and that will have rapid development; and

- Locate point towers only in the highest-density nodes.

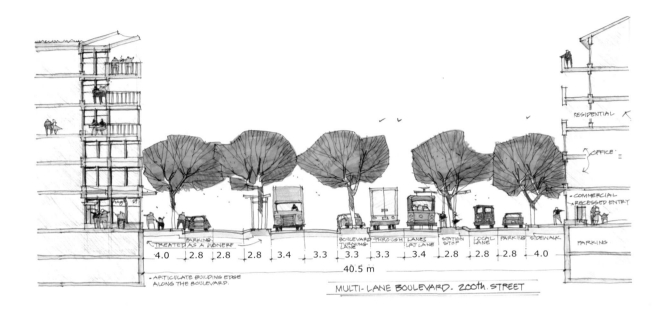

TREATED AS A WONERF

PARKING

BOULEVARD TURNING LANE | THROUGH LANES | LRT LANE | STATION STOP | LOCAL LANE | PARKING | SIDEWALK

RESIDENTIAL

OFFICE

COMMERCIAL RECESSED ENTRY

PARKING

4.0 | 2.8 | 2.8 | 2.8 | 3.4 | 3.3 | 3.3 | 3.3 | 3.4 | 2.8 | 2.8 | 2.8 | 4.0

40.5 m

- ARTICULATE BUILDING EDGE ALONG THE BOULEVARD.

MULTI-LANE BOULEVARD. 200th STREET

GREENWAY GARDENS | PEDESTRIANS TREE ALLEE | BICYCLE | DRAINAGE

3.0 | 3.4 | 3.3 | 3.3 | 3.3 | 3.3 | 3.3 | 3.4

THROUGH LANES | DEDICATED LRT TRANSIT LANE

3.0 | 3.0 | 3.0 | 3.0

15 m

15 m

35 m

200th ST. BOULEVARD & GREENWAY.

Top left:

A multiway boulevard establishes 200th Street as a pedestrian-scale, bicycle-friendly, rapid-transit and major transportation corridor. Two through lanes in each direction — separated by a tree-lined median — continue the length of 200th Street. Development eventually brings enough ridership to support a dedicated express bus/HOV lane and, subsequently, at-grade rapid transit, such as light rail. Within nodes, additional boulevards separate local and parking lanes from through traffic and provide access to abutting commercial and residential uses.

Bottom left:

In residential areas between nodes, wide recreation greenways and stormwater infiltration swales buffer adjacent homes. Rapid transit travels in two additional dedicated through lanes, allowing a slight increase in travel speeds to compensate for slower speeds within nodes. Pedestrian crossings of arterials occur every 400 metres as opposed to every 200 metres in and near nodes.

Below:

As 200th Street is the main access to the Township of Langley from the north, the charrette team designed the street section to have an overall identity that also reflects the character of the nodes through which it passes. At the 72nd node, mixed-use buildings set back from the street create a community green, the new venue for a farmers' market featuring locally grown produce, and give a unique character to the Routley neighbourhood.

mixed use CORRIDORS accessible to all

key charrette conclusions:
high density commercial and residential **corridors** focus growth along transit routes

- Design each key corridor — such as 200th Street — with an overall identity, but reflect neighbourhood character as it moves through and between nodes;

- Envision an at-grade, street-oriented transit system as the heart of 200th Street and of other key multimodal transportation corridors connecting nodes; and

- Use a multiway boulevard and best practices to design pedestrian-scale streets that also function as major commuter and goods movement routes.

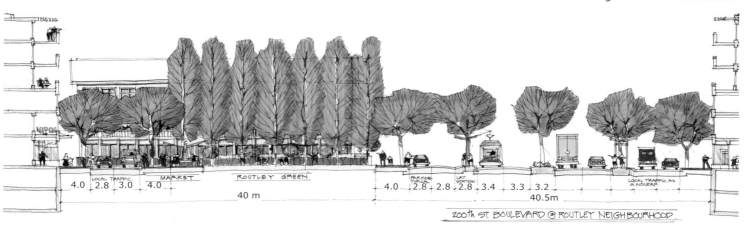

LOCAL TRAFFIC   4.0 | 2.8 | 3.0 | 4.0   MARKET   ROUTLEY GREEN   4.0 | 2.8 | 2.8 | 2.8 | 3.4 | 3.3 | 3.2   LOCAL TRAFFIC AS A MOVER.

40 m   40.5m

200th ST. BOULEVARD @ ROUTLEY NEIGHBOURHOOD.

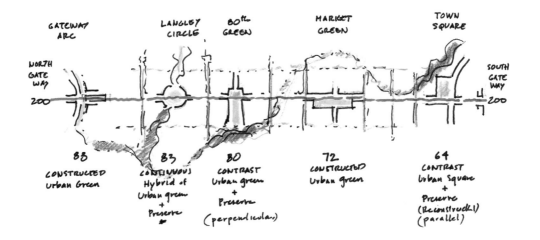

GATEWAY ARC · LANGLEY CIRCLE · 80th GREEN · MARKET GREEN · TOWN SQUARE

NORTH GATE WAY 200

SOUTH GATE WAY 200

85 CONSTRUCTED Urban Green

83 CONTINUOUS Hybrid of Urban green + Preserve

80 CONTRAST Urban green + Preserve (perpendicular)

72 CONSTRUCTED Urban green

64 CONTRAST Urban Square + Preserve (Reconstructed) (parallel)

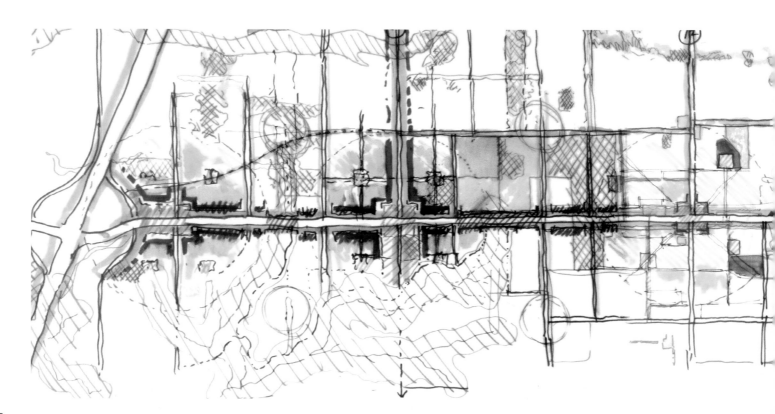

A grid of green pedestrian streets and a sinuous watercourse and trail system connect the nodes, bringing living, working, and playing within walking distance of each other. Streets integrate community greens to emphasize access to adjacent open space and to help draw the landscape into the community fabric. Each node centres on a green, which provides a unique identity and a heart to the walkable neighbourhoods.

Below:

In well-designed communities there are many overlapping nodes with a mix of residential, business, and industrial land uses, placing virtually all residents within a five-minute walk of their daily needs. In this early design concept, the 80th and 86th avenue nodes (at left) are close together, while the 72nd and 64th avenue nodes (at right) are spaced further apart. For the final concept, the 86th Avenue node shifted south to 83rd Avenue to connect the nodes. Over time, smaller nodes will develop between these key nodes, making the length of 200th Street a walkable neighbourhood.

five minute WALKING distance

key charrette conclusions:
interconnected street systems link residents with the services they need

- Create an interconnected street and linear park network so living, working, playing, and transit are within walking distance of each other;

- Provide frequent at-grade crossings of 200th Street and other arterials — a crossing every 200 metres is permitted by the Institute of Transportation Engineers; and

- Design communities that have the edges of nodes close to each other, placing all residents within a five-minute walk of their daily needs.

6.2   3.0   3.3   3.3   3.0
PROMENADE   PARKING   STREET   PARKING
TOWN SQUARE BEHIND.

Top, left:

Streets integrate parks and open space, making them visible. Here, a small traffic diversion redirects vehicles around a circular green space to reveal a Latimer Creek tributary headwater. The depressed circular green collects, filters, and infiltrates stormwater runoff from the surrounding street, highlighting the link between stormwater and healthy streams. Mixed-use and arts buildings wrap the circle, marking this as an important place in the community. The open space network continues across the street.

Top, right:

Places for people to linger are important to a vibrant and lively community. In the 64th Avenue node, Willowbrook Drive — the community's new main shopping street — curves east from 200th Street. Situated on this curve, a new Town Square and Municipal Hall are visible from both directions along the street, creating a strong civic presence. The south-facing square invites people to stop and watch community life.

Bottom, left:

Preserved and rehabilitated riparian areas provide habitat and recreation space for each node. Development fits around these green spaces, which form a contiguous network, connecting residents to natural areas and other neighbourhoods. Areas in which watercourses virtually segregate an area of land (bottom left) are ideal for establishing open field neighbourhood parks that provide a unique and complementary wildlife habitat.

Bottom, right:

Areas without a lot of preserved habitat or with higher development density have revitalized natural areas in many smaller parks. A canal network channels daylighted tributaries and infiltrates stormwater in the 72nd and 64th avenue nodes. This "urban creek" closely fits development patterns and connects small neighbourhood parks. Other open spaces scattered throughout the neighbourhood — at grade and on rooftops — ensure that all residents are only minutes away from a park.

access to NATURAL areas & parks

key charrette conclusions:
green spaces provide recreation opportunities and connect people with **natural systems**

- Make natural areas and parks visible and accessible by drawing these features into the community along linear parks and green streets;

- Fit development around large contiguous areas of preserved open space or natural areas – such as at 80th and 86th avenues at 200th Street; and

- Sprinkle many smaller parks and revitalized natural areas throughout very high-density nodes — such as at 64th Avenue at 200th Street.

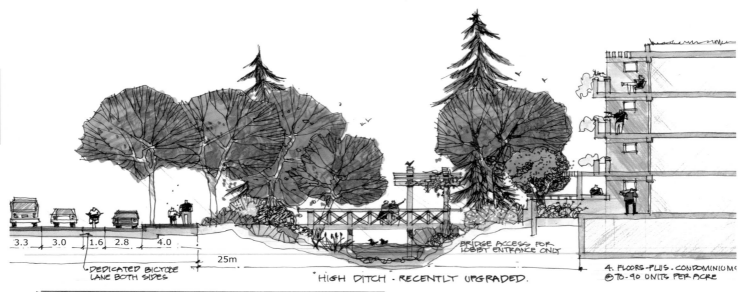

3.3 | 3.0 | 1.6 | 2.8 | 4.0

25m

DEDICATED BICYCLE
LANE BOTH SIDES

BRIDGE ACCESS FOR
LOBBY ENTRANCE ONLY

"HIGH DITCH" · RECENTLY UPGRADED.

4 · FLOORS · PLUS · CONDOMINIUMS
@ 70-90 UNITS PER ACRE

202Bth. STREET. LOOKING SOUTH @ APPROX. 66th.

SCHOOL YARD.

DEDICATED BICYCLE LANE
EACH SIDE.

3.7 | 1.5 1.0 | 2.8 | 3.0 | 3.0 | 3.0 | 3.0 | 2.8 | 1.0 1.5 | 3.7

PARKING | 30m | PARKING

ELEVATE PATIOS · UNITS
ABOVE THE STREET · SIDEWALK

64th. AVENUE · LOOKING EAST.

Top, left:

Langley creeks are important sources of salmon food and habitat. Stormwater from roofs, yards, and streets must continue to infiltrate into the soil, where it can slowly recharge the streams and maintain their health after the community has been developed. Swales in linear parks, at the edge of open space, and along street corridors infiltrate water and also recall the surrounding rural character of the area. In the 64th Avenue node, wide swales provide a buffer between the street and homes, which are accessible from pedestrian bridges.

Bottom left:

The street section provides many environmental benefits. Narrower lanes reduce impervious area, and adjacent swales collect, filter, and infiltrate stormwater from the streets. Multiple rows of street trees contribute to a comfortable pedestrian-scale and micro-environment and reduce the heat island effect. Swales, street trees, and elevated patios buffer adjacent uses from street traffic. Green roofs help to insulate buildings, reduce energy use, and absorb rainfall. Together, these features create streets that are good for people as well as for the environment.

Below:

At regular intervals along the preserved Latimer Creek corridors, biofiltration ponds collect and filter stormwater before it infiltrates the watercourses. Streetside swales from surrounding neighbourhoods feed into these ponds as well as into recreational fields to capture overflow during major rainfall events.

**lighter,
greener,
cheaper,
smarter
INFRASTRUCTURE** Ⓝ

key charrette conclusions:
integrating natural systems reduces **infrastructure** costs and environmental impact

- Use corridors and linear parks to collect stormwater for infiltration;

- Locate biofiltration ponds in parks and around natural areas — particularly creek corridors — to clean stormwater as it recharges groundwater and streams; and

- Design green streets, green roofs, and a dense urban forest canopy to reduce the heat island effect.

Regional Design Charrette

Putting it all together

The case study charrettes provide rules for the urban design of corridors, edges, and nodes. The regional charrette provided the opportunity to show what the region would look like if those rules were used more broadly throughout the region. Does the working hypothesis of this project — that the site is to the region what the cell is to the body — actually hold true? The regional charrette provided the test. But how to conduct that test? Designing an entire region, showing where each and every one of a million new units of housing would go, right down to details of building footprint and set back conditions, would seem impossible at best and quite mad at worst. But without such a demonstration we are subject to the same flaw that has crippled previous efforts at projecting the future of the region. If you resort to methods of depiction that are too general, as, for instance, are the maps that inform the LRSP, then citizens and decision makers end up with no clear idea of how this might change the physical reality of their towns and neighbourhoods. Without an understandable depiction the typical response is fear and rejection. A positive vision of a more complete and sustainable future is required. There is no substitute for a representation detailed enough to allow a clear understanding of the likely consequences in the real world.

The Squares

With no choice then but to take on the whole region, we developed strategies that made this possible. The first strategy had us cutting up the region into five-kilometre by five-kilometre squares, with the resulting grid of squares overlaying the region without reference to municipal or any other kind of boundary. This allowed us to work with manageable pieces and to treat the region as it should be treated: as cultural, economic, and ecological systems extending across the region, with municipal lines exerting little apparent influence on its function. Having made this

decision, we assembled all of our data and resources to conform to this grid. Thus, we laboriously recomputed population and demographic data to conform to these grid cells. The grid cells, therefore, also became the basis for the design program. We assessed each square for its trends of growth in both housing and jobs, and we assigned projections for future job and housing growth (informed both by current trends and by our imperative to keep jobs close to homes).

The rules of the game

Our second challenge: How on earth would we assemble enough skilled practitioners to draw up a credible plan? We estimated that it would take at least 200 person days to design all of the squares. At even modest charge-out rates this would have cost over $200,000. The solution was to hold a massive charrette and to invite 200 people to do the work pro bono all in one day. We were fortunate that, in 2006, Vancouver was playing host to the UN World Urban Forum. This magnet drew the conventions of the Architectural Institute of British Columbia (AIBC)/Royal Architectural Institute of Canada (RAIC), the British Columbia Society of Landscape Architects (BCSLA)/Canadian Society of Landscape Architects (CSLA), and the Planning Institute of British Columbia (PIBC)/Canadian Institute of Planners (CIP) to Vancouver in the same week. From this cadre, nearly 200 volunteered to devote their Saturday to the creation of this plan.

The demographic tidal wave

Our third challenge: who would live here? In 2050 we will be a region of the old. Families with children will only increase by 30 percent, while the number of citizens over sixty-five will increase by nearly 270 percent! We compute that our region has nearly enough family type housing units now. What are needed are over 800,000 units of attached medium- and high-density housing close to services and transit.[1] And it is fortunate that this is the case. Were we to try to put 800,000 single-family homes in our region, we would require as much land as we

presently occupy, forcing the complete consumption of all agricultural land reserve lands and pushing development well into the Fraser Valley.

The Eco-Density Scenario

Finally, it should be noted that there are many assumptions one can make about the region's growth. We made one crucial one: that most of the new growth in the region would occur in the older cities of Vancouver, Burnaby, Coquitlam, and North Surrey. This would not conform with trend growth, which remains more dispersed. We were inspired to make this departure from trend growth because the mayor of Vancouver, Sam Sullivan, in the same month as our regional charrette, launched his "eco-density" initiative, which, in the interests of global sustainability, explicitly called on Vancouver's citizens to accept major increases in density in their neighbourhoods. This initiative accepts the premise that the most important thing you can do to save the planet is to make sure people live as close as they can to their daily needs and, thus, as close together as possible. Inspired by this new vision, we shifted the projected density requirements for each square to be in accordance with it. Thus, the population of Vancouver would double in this scenario to over 1 million citizens.

The key outcomes

There were many discoveries made during the regional charrette, but three stand out. The first is that our region has hundreds of kilometres of corridors that are presently underappreciated and underused and that could be the receptacle for hundreds of thousands of new housing units and millions of square feet of new job and commercial space. Presently occupied by low-intensity single-story structures or parking lots, there are millions of acres of redevelopable space a mere step from frequent transit and services. The second discovery is that so-called suburban office parks are not really so suburban after all. Much has been made of the fact that job growth has occurred outside of town centres in a way that defies expectations embedded in the LRSP. This is true. But on closer examination we see that these office parks are often close to neighbourhoods, services, and transit and could function more sustainably if they were better designed at the site and district scale. Most important, they should better integrate into the fabric of the streets that surround them. The third discovery is that there are myriad opportunities to capture a portion of the value that naturally accrues from hundreds of billions of dollars worth of new development for the gradual reconstruction and rehabilitation of the region's green infrastructure. If we start now with a new and intelligent strategy for reconditioning our streams, parks, and waterways as "green infrastructure," then the doubling of population will produce not a loss of green but a revival of it.

Notes

1 The population and demographic research is condensed in the SxD Foundational Research Bulletins' *Growing a Greater Vancouver Region: Population Scenarios for a Region of 4 Million People* and *Demographic and Housing Projections for a Region of 4 Million*, available at www.sxd.sala.ubc.ca.

Below:

Laying a grid of five-kilometre by five-kilometre squares over the region, without reference to a municipal (or any other kind) of boundary, allowed us to work with more manageable pieces and to treat the region as it should be treated — as consisting of cultural, economic, and ecological systems that are little influenced by municipal lines.

50-year
VISION
Region

key design targets:

The following fifty-year targets for housing and employment informed design deliberations for the region. The targets derive from the findings in the case study charrettes and the SxD foundational research bulletins. Each square had specific targets based on these overall regional targets:

- 2 million new residents with 50 percent of the region's growth within the areas of Vancouver, Burnaby, and New Westminster and 30 percent within the area of northwest Surrey;

- 935,000 new housing units, 15 percent of these being ground-oriented units and 85 percent being apartment type units (percentages differed within the squares); and

- 865,000 new jobs (pursuing a 1:1 ratio of total jobs to total homes in each square).

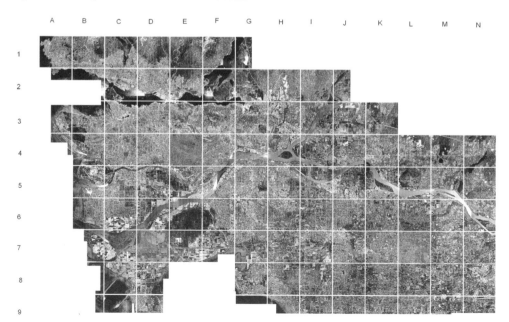

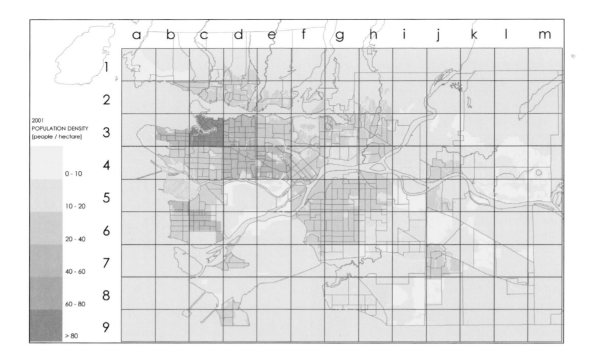

2001
POPULATION DENSITY
[people / hectare]

0 - 10

10 - 20

20 - 40

40 - 60

60 - 80

> 80

PROJECTED
POPULATION DENSITY
[people / hectare]

0 - 10

10 - 20

20 - 40

40 - 60

60 - 80

> 80

Left:

Projecting future population and demographic change is a crucial tool for long-range planning, particularly for land-use decisions that will shape transportation, employment, and housing choices for many decades to come.

Overlaying population-density data and the Green Zone illustrates the region's capacity to accommodate future growth while preserving its environmental assets. At top is the current population density (2001) with the 2056 projected population density for Scenario 3 — the Eco-Density Scenario — shown below. This was the scenario undertaken in the regional design charrette. Population density calculations included all currently developed land as well as undeveloped areas not in the Green Zone.

Right:

In the last twenty years, Greater Vancouver has experienced a population growth of nearly 60 percent, from 1.2 million people in 1981 to almost 2 million in 2001. Similar rates of growth are expected for the future. Fifty years from now, considering the population growth rates from the last twenty years and projecting them over time, we expect the population of Greater Vancouver to be almost 4 million.

Below:

Prior to choosing Scenario 3 for the study, we considered two other projected regional population growth scenarios. The first (below left) — the Trends-Based Scenario — was based on growth rate trends over the last twenty years. The second — the Policy-Based Scenario — modified historic growth trends according to Liveable Region Strategic Plan objectives. All scenarios preserve existing Green Zone and Agricultural Land Reserve lands.

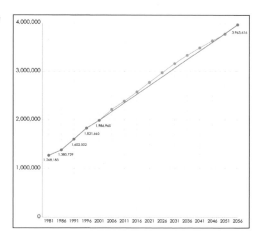

50-year
VISION
Region

key research conclusions:
Population Scenarios for a Region of 4 Million

- Based on historic growth trends over the last twenty years, we expect the population of Greater Vancouver to increase to almost 4 million within a fifty-year time frame;

- The Trends-Based, the Policy-Based, and the Eco-Density scenarios reveal different ways of accommodating population growth throughout the region while preserving the Green Zone; and

- The first key design target for the regional design charrette: 2 million new residents with 50 percent of the region's growth within the area of Vancouver, Burnaby, and New Westminster and 30 percent within the area of northwest Surrey.

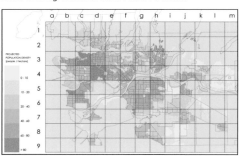

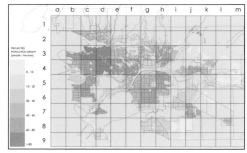

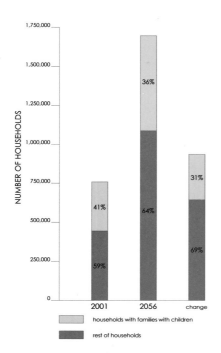

NUMBER OF HOUSEHOLDS

2001 — 41% / 59%
2056 — 36% / 64%
change — 31% / 69%

households with families with children

rest of households

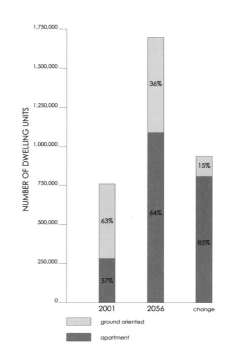

NUMBER OF DWELLING UNITS

2001 — 63% / 37%
2056 — 36% / 64%
change — 15% / 85%

ground oriented

apartment

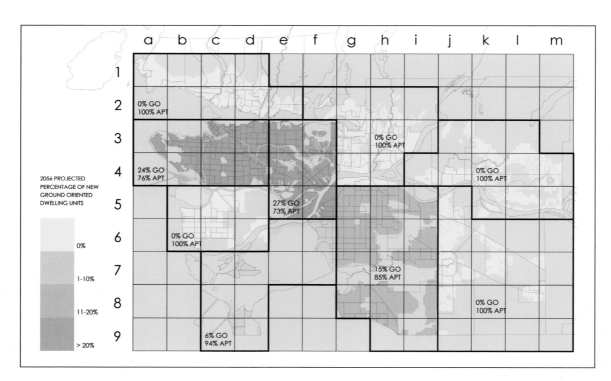

2056 PROJECTED PERCENTAGE OF NEW GROUND ORIENTED DWELLING UNITS

0%
1-10%
11-20%
> 20%

The expected demographic shift will affect both household size (persons per household) and number of households with children. This means demand for dwelling types (ground-oriented versus apartment) will also change. On the one hand, smaller households will require more, but smaller, houses. On the other hand, fewer households with children will require fewer family-sized houses. Together, these changes suggest that, by 2056, ground-oriented single-family units should constitute only 15 percent of new dwelling units in the region, while ground-oriented multifamily and apartment units should make up the remaining 85 percent to accommodate "empty nesters" and "never nesters."

For the Eco-Density scenario, the projected 2056 demographics and current housing mix by subregion determined the expected change in GVRD housing mix between 2001 and 2056, which, in turn, informed the regional design charrette.

Greater Vancouver's population is aging, as is indicated by a rising median age of population and the changing profile by age group, both showing faster growth rates in senior populations than in others. Demographic studies such as BC Stats PEOPLE 27 and Urban Futures' Population Projections suggest that this aging trend will continue in the future, with elder populations making up a dramatically larger share of the total population.

The demographic pyramid below shows population and age cohorts as a percentage of total. The light blue shows the present age and population distribution for the region's 2 million inhabitants. The darker blue shows the projected age and population distribution for 2056 based on Urban Futures projections. The already topheavy demographic becomes extremely weighted towards the elderly with very little growth in the total number of children.

50-year
VISION
Region

key research conclusions:
Demographic and **Housing Projections**
for a Region of 4 Million

- The expected demographic shift will affect future housing needs in terms of decreasing both household size (people per household) and number of households with children. Average persons per household is expected to drop from 2.6 to 2.3. The percentage of families with children in the region is expected to drop from 41 percent to 36 percent;

- A population with a smaller share of households with children combined with the existing ground-oriented housing supply suggests that, by 2056, ground-oriented single-family units should constitute only 15 percent of new dwelling units in the region, with ground-oriented multifamily and apartment units making up the remaining 85 percent to accommodate empty nesters; and

- The second key design target for the regional design charrette: 935,000 new housing units, 15 percent of these being ground-oriented single-family units and 85 percent being ground-oriented multifamily or apartment type units (specific percentages vary within individual squares).

Age group	2006 %	2056 %
65 and over	12.2%	22.5%
55-64	9.1%	13.2%
45-54	15.3%	14.1%
35-44	17.5%	13.7%
25-34	15.0%	13%
20-24	6.8%	5.6%
15-19	6.6%	4.9%
10-14	6.2%	4.6%
5-9	5.9%	4.3%
0-4	5.3%	4.1%

Population and age distribution: 2006
Projected population and age distribution: 2056

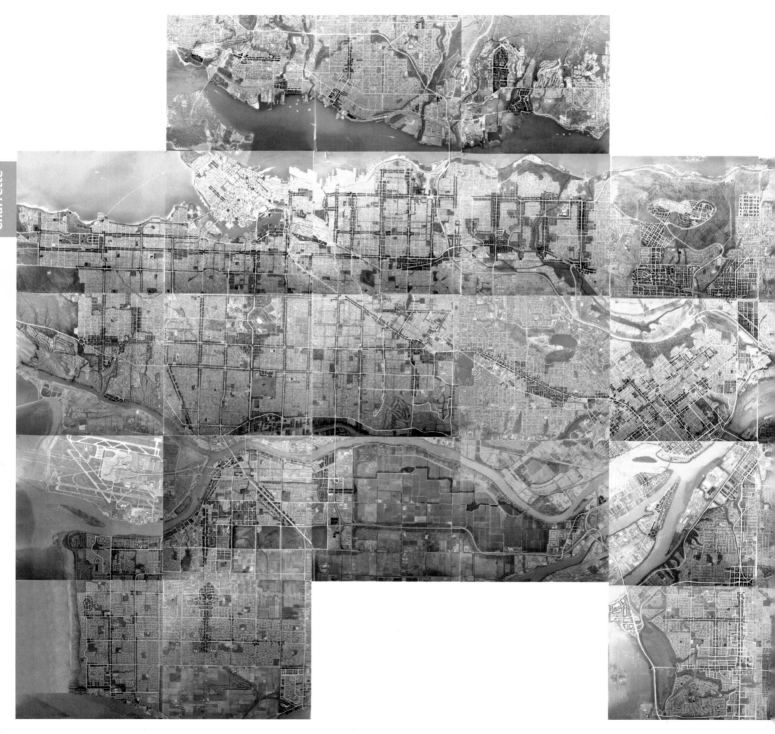

Below:

The regional design charrette applied the project
principles and outcomes of the case study charrettes
to the Greater Vancouver Region in order to create
a vision of a sustainable region of 4 million in 2056.
For six hours participants designed the region to
accommodate a doubling and aging population
and their housing and job needs within sustainable
design principles. Three major findings resulted: the
region contains hundreds of currently underused
corridors with potential capacity to accommodate
new housing, jobs, and commercial space; existing
office parks throughout the region have the capacity
to work sustainably by being better integrated into
the surrounding street fabric; and the region holds
numerous opportunities for "green infrastructure"
development.

**regional design
CHARRETTE
june 17, 2006**

Charrette participants: Ainscough Thomaz, Akolo Akonyo, Aleid Ibrahim, Anton
Suzanne, Arfan Aftab, Avitia Guadalupe, Baird Jim, Baker Brian, Baker Hawke
Kelly, Barrientos Leonal, Belausteguigoitia Jone, Botelho Zita, Braun Heather,
Brown Adrienne, Bula Frances, Cameron Ken, Camray Corwin, Carter Susan,
Carter-Huffman Suzanne, Carvallo Nadia, Chavez Juan, Cherniak Theresa,
Chinwah Chika, Chisholm Blaire, Chiu Paul, Christansen Jeff, Colnett Dianna,
Condon Patrick, Cottrell Rodrey, Craig Carol, Crofton Fiona, Crondahl-Cooper
Cecilia, Culman Sean, Day Dave, De Marco Chris, Dominguez Felipe, Douay
Nicolas, Ducote Frank, Ducote Frank, Ebrahim Zahra, Evans Richard, Freedman
Robert, Fryer Sara, Fung Raymond, Georgejevic Anya, Ghassemi Farzaneh,
Glover Bob, Good Allison, Gradowski Pawel, Grant Robert, Green Jane,
Grinnell Deana, Hallatt Susan, Hallsmith Gwen, Hart Alan, Hartlaub Michelle,
Hemstock Bruce, Henderson Audrey, Hercz Anna, Hester Donald, Hettiarch
Janaki, Hohenschau Dave, Honek Mike, Hornell Mark, Jackson Barb, Jayartyne
Kanake, Jewzyk Stephen, Ji Lin, Johnstone Shana, Kandapola Chamil, Keenan
Eileen, Kerr Doug, Klassen Tony, Klopfer Susanna, Knorr Aaron, Kouneva Alina,
Krueger Paul, Laurenz Jon, Lee Derek, Lee Mark, Leeming Dan, Li Edward, Li
Jia, Lindberg Chris, Luksun Basil, Luksun Basil, Macrae Jane, Mattix Ramana,
McCormick Kathy, McCormick Mike, McCully Al, McGarva Graham, Menard Elise,
Merrill Rick, Mexico Alejandro, Milley Susan, Mitchell Amanda, Mitruen Leo,
Montes Salvador, Mortensen Mike, Mubodean Pascale, Muraki Chisaki, Murphy
Siobhan, Mutashubriwa Phil, Neto Alziro, Newbold Estelle, Newbold Heather,
Nguyen Liz, Nicholls Jamie, Nikolic Diana, Ortiz Cibele, Ouyang Cuining, Palmer
Susan, Panton Ken, Paterson Doug, Pickering Jane, Pohlman Monika, Porter
Edward, Price Gordon, Pritchard Denise, Ramslie Dave, Randall Todd, Redman
Donna, Redman Heidi, Render Brian, Reyes Yolanda, Rodriguez Luis, Rommel
Marina, Romson Mary, Rouleau Greg, Sahai Rajarshi, Sare Kim, Seale Greg,
Semeniuk Xenia, Seni Neha, Singer Saul, Smith Graham, Smith Suzanne, Soni
Neha, Sopeerla Lajra, Spencer Robert, St Pierre Cari, Stefiuk Kate, Stillger
Edward, Straatsma Ray, Talkington Jane, Tanarau Alex, Teed Jackie, Timmer
Jan, Vala Jamie, Van Belleghem Joe, Van Nimwegen Mariken, Venczel Gloria,
Villereal Allegria, Walker Lyle, Wark Robyn, Wawryk Alan, Wei Michael, Wije
Sumana, Winnacott Maxx, Wise David and Yoshida Kate.

Top left:

Mix land uses as much as possible. New neighbourhoods and retrofitted older neighbourhoods should mix housing and commercial uses as much and as closely as possible — even in the same building. At the same time, locating jobs within a maximum five-minute walk from transit (500 metres) considerably reduces car use.

Bottom left:

An aging population requires higher-density homes near transit. Aging shopping centres and their surrounding neighbourhoods are the natural heart of many districts and are ripe for infill with ground-oriented multifamily and apartment units.

Below:

A key research finding: suburban office parks are often located near residential neighbourhoods but lack connection to the surrounding neighbourhood fabric. Office park retrofits that connect to surrounding streets create an interconnected internal street grid, and urban, pedestrian-scale building types can transform these isolated car-oriented job centres into a key element of sustainable communities.

http://www.sxd.sala.ubc.ca/8_research/sxd_TB01_officeparks.pdf

key charrette conclusions:
good & plentiful
JOBS close to home

- Use an internal interconnected street grid that continues into the surrounding neighbourhoods to connect suburban office parks with the community;

- Provide a diversity of uses, mixing housing and commercial uses as much and as closely as possible and even in the same buildings;

- Locate all job areas close to transit, within a maximum five-minute walking distance (500 metres); and

- Use urban building types.

different
HOUSING types

- Provide 800,000 higher-density homes near transit for the projected aging population; and

- Infill aging shopping centres and their surrounding neighbourhoods with a variety of apartment and ground-oriented multifamily housing types as these areas are the natural hearts of many districts and are often ripe for reclaiming.

Left:

By their nature, the corridors in an interconnected grid of streets are accessible. This means that they are an ideal location for jobs, homes, and commercial uses that have easy access to transit. Corridors designed with this ideal in mind are sustainable and can turn an unpleasant urban landscape into a valued one.

Corridors also hold a tremendous capacity to absorb housing above commercial uses and in their immediately surrounding neighbourhoods. Capitalizing on this potential lays the basis for long-term bus and streetcar service efficiencies.

http://www.sxd.sala.ubc.ca/8_research/sxd_TB03_demo_housing.pdf

Below:

Studies show that frequent walking to schools, parks, shops, and transit keeps children and adults healthier. However, in many cases, access to these services is along routes that are unsafe and unpleasant for walking or that are simply disconnected from important destinations. More pedestrian-friendly, interconnected streets combined with frequent bus service within a five-minute walk increases opportunities for walking instead of driving. The circles represent this five minute walk radius.

regional design
CHARRETTE
june 17, 2006

key charrette conclusions:
mixed use
CORRIDORS accessible to all

- Infill housing above commercial uses and in the neighbourhoods immediately surrounding corridors;

- Locate jobs, commercial uses, and housing along corridors to create walkable, sustainable neighbourhoods; and

- Develop sustainable corridors as the basis for long-term bus and streetcar service efficiencies.

five minute
WALKING distance

- Provide frequent bus service within a five-minute walk from all areas, and encourage people to take this walk by making it both pleasant and accessible; and

- Reclaim important but underutilized cross-roads to create a valued centre for presently unfocused neighbourhoods.

Top left:

Development impact fees on new housing can finance reclaiming of degraded green infrastructure. In fifty years complete watershed function could be reclaimed.

Incorporating natural systems into neighbourhoods gives access to riparian areas, provides recreation, and decreases the cost of infrastructure. New housing demands, although met through high density, can be fish and water friendly if they allow at least one inch of rain infiltration per storm event.

Bottom left:

Streets that serve natural drainage, recreation, and alternative modes of movement and that provide habitat transform corridors into a grid of grey and green. Use the existing technology to retrofit older streets and to build new streets to green standards.

regional design
CHARRETTE
june 17, 2006

key charrette conclusions:
access to
NATURAL areas & parks

- Invest in urban areas to provide capital for restoring the green infrastructure;

- Incorporate natural systems into neighbourhoods to provide access to open space and recreation;

- Build high-density residential areas to infiltrate one inch of rain per storm event so that they are fish and water friendly; and

- Green infrastructure should be presented as a network rather than as a collection of occasional events.

lighter, greener, cheaper, smarter
INFRASTRUCTURE

- Reinvest development impact fees from new housing into greening existing grey infrastructure;

- Transform corridor networks into green and grey grids, with streets that provide natural drainage, riparian habitat, trails, and bikeways; and

- Build new streets to green standards using low impact engineering strategies.

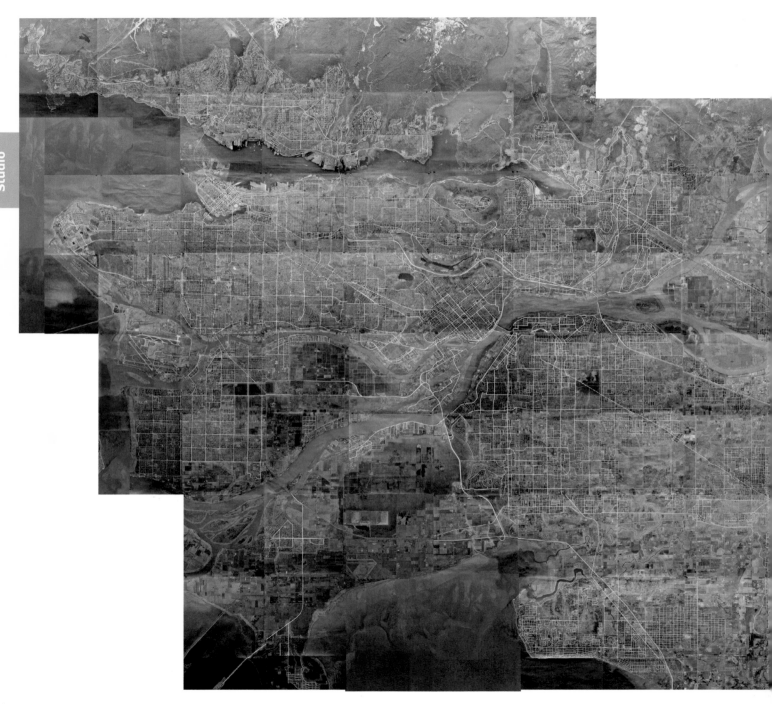

Using the Greater Vancouver Region as the study area, the studio's intent was to provide ideas for a sustainable region and to show the physical implications of these ideas on its neighbourhoods. The idea was to accommodate a doubled population (based on growth rate trends projected over fifty years), with their consequent housing and job needs, while at the same time protecting the Green Zone. Student teams designed five-kilometre by five-kilometre squares, which comprised a map of the region in conformance with sustainability principles discussed in class. By meeting the targets, the studio served as a first iteration field test for the SxD project.

urban design
STUDIO
fall 2005

Fall 2005 Studio Class: Greg Rouleau, Marina Rommel, Jamie Nicholls, Lesya Fesiak, Elise Menard, Mo Rouhi, Xenia Semeniuk, Cecilia Crondall Cooper, Dave Flanders, Yutaka Ikeuchi, Edward Porter, Cuining Ouyang, Jia Li, Niki Strutynski, Qing Xu, Lin Ji, Xue Liu, Ryan Crago, Leigh Sifton, Kate Stefiuk, Sara Fryer, Farzaneh Ghassemi, and Erin Upton.
Instructor: Patrick Condon, Teaching Assistant: Jone Belausteguigoitia

key design targets:

The following fifty-year targets for housing and employment informed design deliberations for the region. Each square had specific targets, along with the following regional targets:

- Incorporate 2 million new residents while protecting the Green Zone;

- Provide 800,000 new housing units (using a 2.5:1 ratio of new people to new homes); and

- Provide 800,000 new jobs (pursuing a 1:1 ratio of total jobs to total homes in each square).

Left:

The resulting ideas and drawings generated en charrette and presented in this book provide a clear and collaboratively produced picture of what a sustainable region of 4 million might look like. If we start now, with a new and intelligent strategy for accommodating future growth and capitalizing on the region's natural assets, a doubled population by 2056 can be the genesis of a region that sustains our children and helps cool the planet